HAND ME ANOTHER BRICK

A Study of Nehemiah

BIBLE STUDY GUIDE
From the Bible-teaching ministry of

Charles R. Swindoll

INSIGHT FOR LIVING

Chuck graduated in 1963 from Dallas Theological Seminary, where he now serves as the school's fourth president, helping to prepare a new generation of men and women for the ministry. Chuck has served in pastorates in three states: Massachusetts, Texas, and California, including almost twenty-three years at the First Evangelical Free Church in Fullerton, California. His sermon messages have been aired over radio since 1979 as the *Insight for Living* broadcast. A best-selling author, Chuck has written numerous books and booklets on many subjects.

Based on the outlines and transcripts of Chuck's sermons, the study guide text is coauthored by Lee Hough, a graduate of the University of Texas at Arlington and Dallas Theological Seminary. He also wrote the Living Insights sections.

Editor in Chief: Cynthia Swindoll
Coauthor of Text: Lee Hough
Assistant Editor: Glenda Schlahta
Copy Manager: Jac La Tour
Copyediting Supervisor: Marty Anderson
Copy Editor: Connie Laser
Production Artists: Gary Lett and Diana Vasquez
Typographer: Bob Haskins
Director, Communications Division: Carla Beck
Project Manager: Alene Cooper
Art Director: Steven Mitchell
Designer: Steven Mitchell
Print Production Manager: Deedee Snyder

Unless otherwise identified, all Scripture references are from the New American Standard Bible, © The Lockman Foundation 1960, 1962, 1963, 1968, 1971, 1972, 1973, 1975, 1977. Used by permission.

An effort has been made to locate sources and obtain permission where necessary for the quotations used in this book. In the event of any unintentional omission, a modification will gladly be incorporated in future printings.

ISBN 1-57972-178-8
Printed in the United States of America

CONTENTS

INTRODUCTION

In a fast-paced, highly competitive world of business procedures and leadership techniques, our hearing a fresh word from God is overdue. How much we need His wisdom!

With each message drawn from the ancient yet timely book of Nehemiah, these studies help us see just how different the drumbeat of Scripture really is. Unlike the dog-eat-dog philosophy of today's strong-willed mentality, Nehemiah models a rare blend of godliness, tact, discipline, determination, grace, and objectivity. You'll admire his remarkable organizational skills and, at the same time, smile with amazement at the way he handles criticism. His project? The building of a wall around Jerusalem. His work force? An unlikely conglomeration of people—some skilled, most not at all—who needed motivation, direction, and encouragement. And that's exactly what he provided . . . in abundance.

May each scriptural lesson assist you in *your* world, with *your* projects, in the midst of all *your* needs today. Apply the wisdom and watch God work. I dare you!

Chuck Swindoll

PUTTING TRUTH INTO ACTION

Knowledge apart from application falls short of God's desire for His children. He wants us to apply what we learn so that we will change and grow. This study guide was prepared with these goals in mind. As you go through the following pages, we hope your desire to discover biblical truth will grow as your understanding of God's Word increases, and that you will be encouraged to apply what you've learned.

To assist you in your study, we've included a section called Living Insights at the end of each lesson. These exercises will challenge you to study further and to think of specific ways to put your discoveries into action.

There are many ways to use this guide—in personal devotions, group studies, discussions with friends and family, and Sunday school classes. And, of course, it's an ideal study aid when you're listening to its corresponding "Insight for Living" radio series.

To benefit most from this study guide, we would encourage you to consider it a spiritual journal. That's why we've included space in the Living Insights for recording your thoughts and discoveries. We hope you'll return to those sections often for review and encouragement as you continue to grow in your walk with Christ.

Lee Hough
Coauthor of Text

HAND ME ANOTHER BRICK

A Study of Nehemiah

Chapter 1

NEHEMIAH:
MAN OF THE HOUR
Survey of Nehemiah

To begin our study today, we must undertake the sensitive business of bringing to mind a treacherous fiend from our past. Someone whose image used to send shivers through our pajamas and have our parents checking closets and underneath beds. Someone so vile, so sneaky, so mean, you were afraid to let your arms or legs dangle over the side of your bed at night, lest he grab them and pull you under. You knew this fang-toothed villain simply as the big bad wolf.

Ooooooo. Who can forget his blustery threat, "Little pig, little pig, let me come in. . . . [Or] I'll huff, and I'll puff, and I'll blow your house in." Of course, the wolf did blow down the homes of the first two little pigs. But, as you may recall, the third little pig had a taste for brick. So he was able to save himself and also provide protection for his brothers, who had less discerning tastes in building materials. And had they followed his lead, they never would have gotten in trouble.

When it comes to leadership qualities, where does your taste run? Do you prefer makeshift philosophies of hay and sticks, or something more brick-solid and enduring from the Rock Himself? If you're tired of living with leadership principles that keep collapsing with the slightest breeze, you need to see Nehemiah. Nehemiah has bricks to offer. Bricks of solid character traits tested in the fiery kiln of experience.

As we study Nehemiah's life, we will see that he had many difficulties and trials come knocking on his door, and he felt the fiery blasts of threats and accusations. But they could not blow him down. Nor could they stop him from leading his people to rebuild Jerusalem's walls, providing protection against the wolves that threatened Israel.

1

Historical Events Related to Nehemiah's Day

Our study of Nehemiah will uncover many bricks of leadership, free for the taking. But in order to fully appreciate them, we need to look back, with the help of the following diagram, at the events and people that shaped Nehemiah's day.

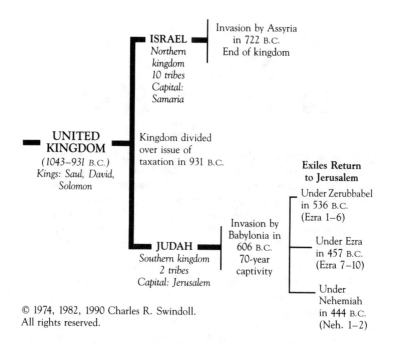

ISRAEL
Northern
kingdom
10 tribes
Capital:
Samaria

Invasion by Assyria
in 722 B.C.
End of kingdom

**UNITED
KINGDOM**
(1043–931 B.C.)
Kings: Saul, David,
Solomon

Kingdom divided
over issue of
taxation in 931 B.C.

JUDAH
Southern kingdom
2 tribes
Capital: Jerusalem

Invasion by
Babylonia in
606 B.C.
70-year
captivity

**Exiles Return
to Jerusalem**

Under Zerubbabel
in 536 B.C.
(Ezra 1–6)

Under Ezra
in 457 B.C.
(Ezra 7–10)

Under
Nehemiah
in 444 B.C.
(Neh. 1–2)

The fountain of all Jewish history flows from one individual, Abraham, whom God promised to make into a great nation. The trickle of Abraham's descendants grew into a roaring flood, taking on worldwide significance as a united kingdom under the reigns of Saul, David, and Solomon. During the latter years of Solomon's reign, however, his moral compromises became so great that God finally judged him.

> So the Lord said to Solomon, "Because you have done this, and you have not kept My covenant and My statutes, which I have commanded you, I will surely tear the kingdom from you, and will give it to your servant. Nevertheless I will not do it in your days for the sake of your father David, but I will tear it out of the hand of your son." (1 Kings 11:11–12)

And in 931 B.C., Solomon's son caused an irreconcilable split in the waters of his people. The current of the ten northern tribes pulled away to form their own nation, using the name Israel. The two remaining tribes in the south bore the name Judah.

The idolatry fostered by Israel's corrupt leadership for the next 209 years completely desecrated the spiritual wellsprings of its people. In 722 B.C. God dried up this polluted branch of Abraham's offspring, using the conquering Assyrians as His tool of judgment.

The flow of Judah's history continued for another 134 years after Israel's downfall, and then it, too, was judged for its spiritual impurity. This time the Babylonians, led by King Nebuchadnezzar, were the instruments of God's wrath.

> Therefore He brought up against them the king of the Chaldeans who slew their young men with the sword in the house of their sanctuary, and had no compassion on young man or virgin, old man or infirm; He gave them all into his hand. And all the articles of the house of God, great and small, and the treasures of the house of the Lord, and the treasures of the king and of his officers, he brought them all to Babylon. Then they burned the house of God, and broke down the wall of Jerusalem and burned all its fortified buildings with fire, and destroyed all its valuable articles. And those who had escaped from the sword he carried away to Babylon; and they were servants to him and to his sons until the rule of the kingdom of Persia. (2 Chron. 36:17–20)

After an appointed time of seventy years, God shifted the world power from the Babylonians to the Persians and Medes. He then prompted the new captors to allow the Jews to return to their homeland. First King Cyrus, and later Artaxerxes, allowed the Jews to return home to pick up the pieces of their ravaged lives and homeland (2 Chron. 36:22–23, Ezra 7:11–13). The first band to return was led by Zerubbabel in 536 B.C.; nearly eighty years later another band returned under the leadership of Ezra in 457 B.C.; and a final group, led by Nehemiah, returned thirteen years following, in 444 B.C.

The trickle of Jews from the first two exoduses began refilling their dry homeland. Ezra led the people to revive their spiritual lives and rebuild the temple in Jerusalem. But the protective walls surrounding the city were still as Nebuchadnezzar had left them—in ruins.

This brings us to Nehemiah's book. The first three verses open with the arrival of some visitors who pour out some disturbing news to Nehemiah about Jerusalem.

> "The remnant there in the province who survived the captivity are in great distress and reproach, and the wall of Jerusalem is broken down and its gates are burned with fire." (Neh. 1:3)

Now that we have followed the thread of history that ties into our study, let's take a moment to survey the man who will guide us through the rest of our lesson—Nehemiah.

Nehemiah: Man of the Hour

To gain an understanding of Nehemiah, we need to briefly look at the three successive roles he plays in this book—those of cupbearer, builder, and governor.

Nehemiah: The Cupbearer

The first role we find Nehemiah playing is cupbearer to King Artaxerxes of Persia (v. 11). Far from being an insignificant slave, the cupbearer "in ancient oriental courts was always a person of rank and importance. From the confidential nature of his duties and his frequent access to the royal presence, he possessed great influence."[1]

It was during this time of service to the king that Nehemiah received the news concerning Jerusalem's walls. Instead of rushing in to petition the king for help, however, Nehemiah first took his petitions to the King of Kings (vv. 4–11).

Eventually, Nehemiah's countenance began to reflect the strain of carrying such a burden in his heart.

> And it came about in the month Nisan, in the twentieth year of King Artaxerxes, that wine was before him, and I took up the wine and gave it to the king. Now I had not been sad in his presence. So the king said to me, "Why is your face sad though you are not sick? This is nothing but sadness of heart." Then I was very much afraid. And I said to the king, "Let the king live forever. Why should my face not be sad when the city, the place of my fathers' tombs, lies desolate and its gates have been consumed by fire?"

---

1. Merrill F. Unger, *Unger's Bible Dictionary*, 3d ed. (Chicago, Ill.: Moody Press, 1966), see "Cupbearer."

Then the king said to me, "What would you request?" So I prayed to the God of heaven. (2:1–4)

The moment that Nehemiah's prayers had prepared him for had arrived, and he was ready.

> And I said to the king, "If it please the king, and if your servant has found favor before you, send me to Judah, to the city of my fathers' tombs, that I may rebuild it." Then the king said to me, the queen sitting beside him, "How long will your journey be, and when will you return?" So it pleased the king to send me, and I gave him a definite time. (vv. 5–6)

With the king's permission, Nehemiah laid aside his cupbearer's robes and put on a hard hat to assume his new role as Nehemiah the builder.

Nehemiah: The Builder

Upon arriving in Jerusalem, Nehemiah's first task was to inspect the ruins of the wall, from which he would formulate his construction plans.

> And I arose in the night, I and a few men with me. I did not tell anyone what my God was putting into my mind to do for Jerusalem and there was no animal with me except the animal on which I was riding. So I went out at night by the Valley Gate in the direction of the Dragon's Well and on to the Refuse Gate, inspecting the walls of Jerusalem which were broken down and its gates which were consumed by fire. Then I passed on to the Fountain Gate and the King's Pool, but there was no place for my mount to pass. So I went up at night by the ravine and inspected the wall. Then I entered the Valley Gate again and returned. (vv. 12–15)

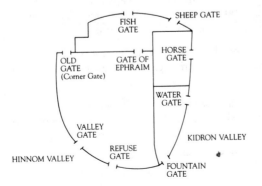

5

After his moonlight survey, Nehemiah was finally ready to bring his plans out into the open (vv. 17–18).

Chapters 3–5 tell us, through Nehemiah's eyes, of the work that was carried on in spite of the great odds, obstacles, and enemies the people encountered. Finally the prayers, the planning, and the people's hard work culminated in a protective wall (6:15)—after more than ninety years of lying in ruins.

Nehemiah: The Governor

Beginning with chapter 7, Nehemiah lays his hard hat aside to take up the keys to the city and begin functioning in his appointed role as governor (see 5:14).

Immediately, Nehemiah begins commissioning spiritual men to occupy places of authority in the city (7:1–2). He reestablishes the practice of God's laws and commemorative feasts in the community. The public reading of the Law of Moses is given, temple worship is restored, and Nehemiah succeeds in purifying his people by removing all foreign influences (13:30).

Wall Rebuilding Then . . . Wall Rebuilding Now

Ancient walls like Jerusalem's served many functions. They offered protection and security and reflected the strength of the people. They also made it possible for the people to cultivate their spiritual lives nationally as well as individually without outside interference.

Likewise, the walls of spiritual disciplines that we build around our lives are vital for our protection and for cultivating a relationship with the Lord. Before we enter into Nehemiah's struggle to rebuild Jerusalem's walls, maybe some of us need to examine the status of our own spiritual walls. Are there some gates that have been left open for the enemy to slip through? Has neglect allowed a loose piece of stone or mortar to become a hole, a gap? Have the weeds of compromise overrun certain sections until those toppled walls have become main thoroughfares for yesterday's unthinkable rebellions?

If your walls are in need of repair, whether just a brick or two or whole sections, take a moment now to apply some principles from Nehemiah's life.

First: *Develop a genuine concern for the condition of the walls.* The project to restore the walls of Jerusalem did not begin when the people began laying new bricks. It began as a burden in one man's heart. Like Nehemiah, we must have a genuine concern for the condition of our walls.

6

Second: *Express direct prayer for guidance and protection.* Before he ever began to rebuild the wall, Nehemiah started working on it from eight hundred miles away—in prayer before the Lord. For many of us, prayer is too often an afterthought, something rattled off at ribbon cuttings when the work has already been done. Get in the habit of acting on your burdens only *after* you have given them a firm foundation of prayer.

Third: *Face the situation honestly and with determination until the task is finished.* When Nehemiah met with the people in Jerusalem, he didn't attempt to gloss over the true condition of the wall. Instead, he pointed it out clearly (2:17). For only through an honest appraisal could he secure the kind of steadfast commitment it would take to see the job finished. Likewise, without honest appraisals of the conditions of our own spiritual walls, we will always be running out of determination before the gaps are filled.

Fourth: *Recognize that we cannot correct the condition alone.* Our natural tendency is to revert to a spiritual wilderness; no amount of bricklaying experience can thwart sin's power to crumble our walls. It is only when we are willing to live in dependence upon God that we'll have the power to erect the spiritual walls we need for survival.

Living Insights

Breezes aren't pushy like gusts; they don't try to overwhelm you like gales. No, the gentle urgings of breezes are more like caresses that imperceptibly leave you leaning in their direction.

Oftentimes, the most difficult and dangerous sins we encounter are like breezes. There are no wind warning flags stirring, no violent destructive blasts to resist. Only subtle wafts of sin in the skillful hands of the tempter, lulling us to drop our guard . . . neglect our spiritual walls.

For the next few minutes, in stillness before God, pray for His help in recognizing those breezes in your life that are causing you to drift into moral compromises. Write them down. Then draft some specific plans to seal up the cracks in your spiritual walls before they crumble.

Lulling Breezes

_____   _____

_____   _____

Plan of Reinforcement

_____

_____

_____

_____

_____

_____

_____

_____

_____

_____

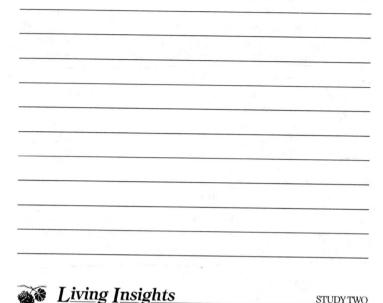 ## _Living Insights_   STUDY TWO

An old Disney cartoon classic you may remember opens with a syrupy, mild-mannered fellow leaving his home in the morning for work. Everything is happy and serene. He's a model citizen . . . until he gets behind the wheel of his car. At that moment he becomes a crazed, diabolical fiend as he careens his way to work.

The cartoonists must have had a good laugh in creating that one, because it hits so close to reality. All of us have those areas in our lives where our serene characters grow fangs.

Like Nehemiah, we all face the challenge of making sure that our beliefs are faithfully applied in each of the roles God places us in. For Nehemiah, that meant being faithful as a cupbearer, builder, and governor. What about you? Are you the same person in church that you are in the car on the way home? How about in the office, at play, on business trips, at home with the family? Or are you a spiritual chameleon—your faith changing with each different role?

Not only over a lifetime, but each day, we are required to faithfully live out several roles. Is there a particular one that needs your attention right now? Take a moment to reflect on this. Then try to write down a strategy for making that role more pleasing to the Lord.

Your Strategy

_____

_____

_____

_____

_____

_____

_____

_____

_____

_____

_____

_____

_____

Chapter 2

NEHEMIAH
ON HIS KNEES

Nehemiah 1:1–11

Sometimes the answers to weighty questions such as, What is leadership? are most easily found in the unsophisticated world of children.

For example, remember how leadership struggles were resolved by the neighborhood gang when you were little? You tried to woo everyone with, "Come to my house and play and you'll get cake and ice cream!" And the wide-eyed group of followers, now a powerful constituency, anxiously turned to hear the challenger's bid: "Oh yeah? Well, my mom just finished makin' some biiig chocolate chip cookies—*and*—you can all ride my horse." And that settled the leadership crisis. His horse trumped your cake. The barefoot electorate voted with a unanimous whoop and stampeded for the new leader's hacienda. You started to say something about your dad having a jet, but it was too late—Jesse James and his gang were already long gone.

When you apply the question What is leadership? to that scene, one word comes to mind—*influence*. You lead people according to the measure that you influence them. From neighborhood politics to world politics, the same one-word definition of leadership holds true. As President Harry Truman once said, "A leader is a person who has the ability to get others to do what they don't want to do, and like it."[1] Crossing over from the political to the military, we see that Field Marshal Montgomery defined *leadership* as "the capacity and will to rally men and women to a common purpose, and the character which inspires confidence."[2] Leaders from all different fields, nations, and neighborhoods agree: the stronger the influence, the stronger the leadership.

But how do we gain that influence? By offering the most cake and ice cream? Relying on manipulation techniques? Carrying the biggest club? Screaming the loudest?

1. As quoted by J. Oswald Sanders in *Spiritual Leadership*, rev. ed. (Chicago, Ill.: Moody Press, 1980), p. 36.

2. As quoted by Sanders in *Spiritual Leadership*, p. 35.

People have tried them all, and they all fall short of God's design for leading. Only one method moves and influences people the way a true leader should. Hudson Taylor put into words what Nehemiah is going to show us, "It is possible to move men, through God, *by prayer alone.*"[3]

Nehemiah 1—A Prelude of Prayer

A study of the book of Nehemiah is a study on leadership. It is a stockpile of solid leadership bricks that can be built into your life. In this first chapter Nehemiah offers the cornerstone on which the Christian leader's influence rests—prayer.

Orientation

Without any fanfare, Nehemiah identifies himself as the book's author and as King Artaxerxes' cupbearer (vv. 1, 11). In this trusted position as the food-and-wine taster, Nehemiah acted as a protective screen between the public and the king.

In addition, we are told that the action starts in the month Chislev, meaning December, in the "twentieth year." Whenever you lived under a monarchy, new life started when the new king started. If you lived in the second year of the king, all dates would be given as being in the second year. In Nehemiah's case, he was living in the twentieth year of King Artaxerxes' reign, about 444 B.C.

Finally, we're told that he was in Susa, the capital not only of Persia, but of the ancient world.

Situation

Most of us know what it's like to get hit with situations that come without warning, sending our lives spinning in an unexpected direction. In verse 2 Nehemiah begins relating the situation that knocked him out of his normal routine.

> Hanani, one of my brothers, and some men from Judah came; and I asked them concerning the Jews who had escaped and had survived the captivity, and about Jerusalem.

Nehemiah may have lived in the Persian capital, but the capital of his heart was Jerusalem.

> And they said to me, "The remnant there in the province who survived the captivity are in great distress

---

3. As quoted by Sanders in *Spiritual Leadership*, p. 110.

and reproach, and the wall of Jerusalem is broken down
and its gates are burned with fire." (v. 3)

Here Nehemiah's heartfelt longings collide with the reality pictured by the witnesses. In Hebrew *great distress* means "misery, calam-
ity"; *reproach* means "sharp, cutting, penetrating, piercing." You
want the plain truth, Nehemiah? The people in your hometown are
in a calamitous, miserable, and depressed situation. They are being
criticized and harassed by their enemies, they live in constant fear of
attack, and their lives are like the walls that surround them, in ruins.

Reaction

The first three verses in this great concerto on leadership are
played in a minor key. The introductory tones of verse 1 quickly
segue into the dissonant news of the remnant in verses 2 and 3.
Together, this overture of sorrowful strains strikes a deep, resonant
chord of leadership in Nehemiah that flows out in an arpeggio of
verbs: "I heard . . . sat down . . . wept . . . mourned . . . was fasting . . . praying" (v. 4).

Within the main melody, verses 4–11, there are four movements,
each highlighting qualities that are true in the lives of spiritual
leaders.

First: *He had a clear recognition of the need.* The beginnings of the
first movement are barely audible in the simple opening words, "It
came about when I heard these words" (v. 4a). Although Nehemiah
worked in a palace, he would not allow his heart or mind the luxury
of ivory-tower preoccupations. He was not afraid of the truth, not
afraid to see the problems. Especially when it came to hearing about
the needs of those closest to his heart.[4]

Second: *He was personally concerned with the need.* The low, understanding tones of the first movement suddenly give way to a thunder-
ous volume billowing into clouds of remorse: "I sat down and wept
and mourned for days" (v. 4a). The tempo flashes and a steady
shower of intense feelings ensues: "I was fasting and praying before
the God of heaven" (v. 4b). Nehemiah allowed the anguish and
misery of his people to pierce his heart. And from that wound the
mournings of his people, mixed with his own, were poured out
before the Lord. Alan Redpath, in his book on Nehemiah, writes:

---

4. By way of contrast, in 1 Samuel 2:12–16 and 3:1–13 we have an example of a
father who refused to recognize the need. According to 3:13 Eli knew of the sinful
behavior of his sons, but he did not rebuke them. As a result, God brought judgment
on his home. Are you willing to recognize the needs in your life?

Let us learn this lesson from Nehemiah: you never lighten the load unless you first have felt the pressure in your own soul. You are never used of God to bring blessing until God has opened your eyes and made you see things as they are. There is no other preparation for Christian work than that. Nehemiah was called to build the wall, but first he had to weep over the ruins.[5]

The typical response would have been to blame the people, "They've been back for how long and still haven't built that wall? Who's in charge?" But in Nehemiah's response there are no discordant notes of blame, only the resonant notes of compassion.

Third: *He went to God first with the need.* The third movement picks up on the final, sweeping crescendo of verse 4: "praying before the God of heaven." This will guide us through one of Nehemiah's intense refrains of intercession (vv. 5–11).

Here the genius of Nehemiah's leadership is displayed. He resists the normal temptation to pick up the conductor's baton and orchestrate the wall's reparation himself. Instead, he goes to his knees, beseeching the One whose place it is to conduct all the affairs of men and meld their efforts into one harmonious plan.

Let's briefly analyze the sections that blend together to form Nehemiah's prayer. First, he expresses *praise.*

> And I said, "I beseech Thee, O Lord God of heaven, the great and awesome God, who preserves the covenant and lovingkindness for those who love Him and keep His commandments." (v. 5)

Nehemiah's praise immediately begins clearing his mind of any distracting fears. He is reminded that he need not fear the shadow of the world's mightiest king when he's under the shadow of the Almighty.

Next, he offers *confession.*

> "Let Thine ear now be attentive and Thine eyes open to hear the prayer of Thy servant which I am praying before Thee now, day and night, on behalf of the sons of Israel Thy servants, confessing the sins of the sons of Israel which we have sinned against Thee; I and my father's house have sinned. We have acted very corruptly against Thee and have not kept the commandments,

5. Alan Redpath, *Victorious Christian Service: Studies in the Book of Nehemiah* (Westwood, N.J.: Fleming H. Revell Co., 1958), pp. 19–20.

nor the statutes, nor the ordinances which Thou didst command Thy servant Moses." (vv. 6–7)

Notice that Nehemiah uses the words *we* and *I*. Rather than focusing on someone else's wrongs, he confesses his own failings that have contributed to the problem.

In the third section, Nehemiah claims God's *promise*.

> "Remember the word which Thou didst command Thy servant Moses, saying, 'If you are unfaithful I will scatter you among the peoples; but if you return to Me and keep My commandments and do them, though those of you who have been scattered were in the most remote part of the heavens, I will gather them from there and will bring them to the place where I have chosen to cause My name to dwell.' And they are Thy servants and Thy people whom Thou didst redeem by Thy great power and by Thy strong hand." (vv. 8–10)

Using the stored-up Scriptures in his heart, Nehemiah reminds God of the promise He made to Israel in the days of Moses (see Lev. 26:33, Deut. 30:1–5).

The final section of Nehemiah's prayer climaxes with *petition*. The ground swell of praise, confession, and claiming God's promises have all been building up to this pointed request:

> "O Lord, I beseech Thee, may Thine ear be attentive to the prayer of Thy servant and the prayer of Thy servants who delight to revere Thy name, and make Thy servant successful today, and grant him compassion before this man." (Neh. 1:11)

Nehemiah's request for success doesn't mean "Make me rich." Rather he was seeking the kind of success that comes from accomplishing God's will on earth.

Fourth: *He was available to meet the need.* With this fourth movement, our concerto of leadership qualities comes to its finale. A finale that not only concludes our study of the first chapter but also opens a door to the second.

Amid the climactic strains of Nehemiah's petition (v. 11), an essential leadership quality emerges—*availability*. But in order to be available to meet the need of rebuilding the wall, Nehemiah must first overcome a hurdle—"this man," King Artaxerxes. Which brings us back to the opening premise of our study: "It is possible to move men, through God, *by prayer alone.*"

14

Practical Conclusion for Today

Possibly the most penetrating of all the New Testament books is the letter from James, an apostle who was otherwise known in the first century as "camel knees." He received this nickname because he constantly knelt in prayer. His knees became knobby, knotty, and thick until they literally bagged like a camel's.[6]

What would your nickname be when it comes to prayer? "Prayer warrior" or "prayerless worrier"? Let me leave you with these four reasons why prayer is important. First, it makes us wait. We can't earnestly pray and, at the same time, rush out ahead of God. We have to wait till we finish praying. Second, it clears our vision. It enables us to see situations through God's eyes and not our own. Third, it quiets our hearts. We cannot continue to worry and pray at the same time. One will weed out the other, depending on which one we choose. Fourth, it activates our faith. And with that faith comes an attitude of hope and peace which replaces the petty and critical attitude that comes when we haven't prayed.

Living Insights   STUDY ONE

Imagine for a moment that the following quote from Tennyson's *Idylls of the King* came to you in the form of a letter.

Dear _____,
        (fill in your name)

> If thou shouldst never see my face again,
> Pray for my soul. More things are wrought by prayer
> Than this world dreams of. Wherefore, let thy voice
> Rise like a fountain for me night and day.
> For what are men better than sheep or goats
> That nourish a blind life within the brain,
> If, knowing God, they lift not hands of prayer
> Both for themselves and those who call them friend?
> For so the whole round earth is every way
> Bound by gold chains about the feet of God.[7]

                                        Signed _____

---

6. *The Zondervan Pictorial Encyclopedia of the Bible* (Grand Rapids, Mich.: Zondervan Publishing House, 1976), see "James, 'the Lord's brother.'"

7. Alfred, Lord Tennyson, "The Passing of Arthur," *Idylls of the King*, ed. Willis Boughton (Boston, Mass.: Ginn and Co., 1913), p. 155.

Who sent you that letter? Who is it that wants, *needs*, your leadership right now in the way of prayer? A spouse? Your children? Someone you work with? Sign the letter with their name, as if you were making a covenant to influence them through God—by prayer alone.[8]

Living Insights STUDY TWO

Nehemiah listened. This may not sound all that important, but in our fast-paced society, people who listen are becoming an endangered species. Many of us are so busy "getting by" or "making it to the top" that other people are only a blur of sight and sound. There's no time for listening to the burdens of others. We're told that these people only slow us down, complicate things, infringe on our freedom—especially the very young and old. People who listen, like poet Shel Silverstein's little old man, are rare indeed.

> Said the little boy, "Sometimes I drop my spoon."
> Said the little old man, "I do that too."
> The little boy whispered, "I wet my pants."
> "I do that too," laughed the little old man.
> Said the little boy, "I often cry."
> The old man nodded, "So do I."
> "But worst of all," said the boy, "it seems
> Grown-ups don't pay attention to me."
> And he felt the warmth of a wrinkled old hand.
> "I know what you mean," said the little old man.[9]

Nehemiah listened, and that led to a king being moved, a wall being built, and a whole city being revitalized in its worship of God.

Now, take a moment to slowly read Matthew 25:31–46.

Have you heard the Savior lately? How are your listening skills? That's a hard one to pin down sometimes, so here are a few questions to help you. Do you usually formulate your opinion before someone finishes talking? Do you have a tendency to finish other people's sentences for them? Do you focus your attention on the person

8. For help in learning how to develop your prayer life, read Dr. William E. Sangster's booklet *Teach Me to Pray* (Nashville, Tenn.: Upper Room, 1959) or Ray C. Stedman's *Talking to My Father: What Jesus Teaches on Prayer,* Authentic Christianity Books Series (Portland, Oreg.: Multnomah Press, 1985).

9. Shel Silverstein, "The Little Boy and the Old Man," *A Light in the Attic,* p. 95. © 1981 Evil Eye Music, Inc. Reprinted by permission of Harper and Row, Publishers, Inc.

talking, or are you easily distracted? Do you rely on anger to force people to do what you want because it's easier and quicker than having to really listen?

It might get messy if you listen. You might hear and see some things that will sicken and sorrow you as they did Nehemiah. Are you willing to take that risk? Have you heard the Savior lately?

Chapter 3

PREPARATION FOR A MIGHTY TASK

Nehemiah 2:1–11

Have you ever worked for a boss of the *Tyrannosaurus rex* species—that carnivorous, flesh-eating kind that loves to prey on powerless herbivorous subordinates? These tyrants roam in the hierarchy of every field of endeavor: education, the military, corporations, churches, medicine, politics, even the home. Today's power-behemoths devour people's spirits instead of their flesh. They attack with the sharp, serrated teeth of sarcasm, criticism, threats, and belittling comments, shredding their victim's self-esteem.

Unfortunately, those bilious leaders with the *savoir faire* of bull nettle are a part of most everyone's landscape. Which leaves all of us in one of three categories: those who have had trouble with their bosses, those who are now having trouble, and those who will have trouble!

An appropriate subtitle for today's lesson could be "How to Handle a Difficult Boss." In it we'll watch Nehemiah handle the *Tyrannosaurus rex* of his day, Artaxerxes, who also happened to be *his* boss.

In our last lesson, one banner of truth stood out above all others: "It is possible to move men, through God, *by prayer alone.*"[1] Nehemiah employed the only effective tool he had for moving a boss he was powerless to change—prayer. It was a tool he may have learned to use from Solomon.

A Principle from Proverbs

> The king's heart is like channels of water in the hand
> of the Lord. (Prov. 21:1a)

The word *channels* refers to canals or irrigation ditches that run in various directions from a main source of water. Literally translated, the first part of this verse would read, "Like irrigation canals of water is the heart of a king in the hand of Jehovah." The writer is saying that the heart of the king, where all decisions are made, is in the hands of the Lord.

---

1. Hudson Taylor, as quoted by J. Oswald Sanders in *Spiritual Leadership*, rev. ed. (Chicago, Ill.: Moody Press, 1980), p. 110.

The second half of this proverb comes in the form of a declaration: "He turns it wherever He wishes" (v. 1b). Whether the king is saved or unsaved, God determines the direction the decisions of his heart will flow. The words "He turns it" are more vividly pictured in the Hebrew as "He causes it to bend." Putting it all together, the verse would read like this:

> Like irrigation canals carrying water, so is the heart of
> the king in Jehovah's hand. He causes it to bend and
> incline in whatever direction He pleases.

This verse from Proverbs 21 is a perfect prologue to the drama in Nehemiah 2. We know from the last verse of chapter 1 that Nehemiah was the cupbearer to a dictator known for his rigid and stubborn will—a tough boss. The distressing news of Jerusalem's fallen walls raised in Nehemiah an urgent desire—to rebuild his city's protection. But he knew Artaxerxes was unlikely to give him leave.[2] So he did the only thing he could do. He started praying.

Nehemiah in Persia

Through Nehemiah's personal account, we're given front-row seats in a dramatization of Proverbs 21:1, the King moving a king.

Time and Setting

The action in Nehemiah 2 is set in the month of Nisan, or April. Tucked silently between this writing and the writing of chapter 1 in December are four anguishing months of prayer and waiting.

In verse 1 we see Nehemiah fulfilling his normal duties as cup-bearer, but today there is something different about him. Despite the opulence, privilege, and prestige of his position under Artaxerxes, Nehemiah can no longer hide the sorrow that rules his inner world.

> And it came about in the month Nisan, in the
> twentieth year of King Artaxerxes, that wine was be-
> fore him, and I took up the wine and gave it to the king.
> [Until] now I had not been sad in his presence. (v. 1)

Conversation and Decision

In the next 6½ verses Nehemiah records what is known as an *interchange*—the back-and-forth conversation between him and the

---

2. "Nehemiah's task is . . . hard because he desires permission to return to Jerusalem and rebuild the wall—the specific thing which Artaxerxes had previously forbidden (Ezra 4:17–22)." Cyril J. Barber, *Nehemiah and the Dynamics of Effective Leadership* (Neptune, N.J.: Loizeaux Brothers, 1976), p. 29.

king as it actually took place. Like a dramatic actor lending life to the lines of a printed script, Nehemiah intensifies the meaning of this dialogue by candidly inserting his emotional responses. In doing so, he builds on the pall of sadness we know hangs over the scene. Let's listen in as the conversation unfolds.

> So the king said to me, "Why is your face sad though you are not sick? This is nothing but sadness of heart." Then I was very much afraid. (v. 2)

The king's words pass through Nehemiah's heart like a chilling wind—it is a crime punishable by death to have a sad countenance, for it might suggest dissatisfaction with the king. Nehemiah chooses his next words carefully.

> And I said to the king, "Let the king live forever. Why should my face not be sad when the city, the place of my fathers' tombs, lies desolate and its gates have been consumed by fire?" Then the king said to me, "What would you request?" (vv. 3–4a)

In the unseen world of the king's heart, there is the unmistakable sound of rushing water swirling past a dike that is beginning to crumble. The cupbearer recognizes who is at work.

> So I prayed to the God of heaven. And I said to the king, "If it please the king, and if your servant has found favor before you, send me to Judah, to the city of my fathers' tombs, that I may rebuild it." Then the king said to me, the queen sitting beside him, "How long will your journey be, and when will you return?" So it pleased the king to send me, and I gave him a definite time. (vv. 4b–6)

Reflected in the king's questions is a deep appreciation for Nehemiah and his work—he wants the cupbearer to come back. This says something important about Nehemiah. Although his heart longs for Jerusalem, he has carried out his duties in this foreign land with the same meticulous care he would have given them in his homeland (see Col. 3:22–25).

Tacked on to the end of that block of Scripture, in the words "and I gave a definite time," is an important leadership quality: the ability to plan and organize. Nehemiah's well-thought-out itinerary came from planning his way through the whole project while prayerfully waiting on God to move Artaxerxes. Going out in faith doesn't mean you go out haphazardly without any plans. Jesus himself warned:

"Don't begin until you count the cost. For who would begin construction of a building without first getting estimates and then checking to see if he has enough money to pay the bills? Otherwise he might complete only the foundation before running out of funds. And then how everyone would laugh! 'See that fellow there?' they would mock. 'He started that building and ran out of money before it was finished!'"
(Luke 14:28–30)[3]

Nehemiah had counted the cost and was prepared to complete the construction of the wall, from its foundation to its highest parapets.

Result and Reason

In the few moments it has taken for this conversation to transpire, Nehemiah has already switched roles from cupbearer to general contractor. He immediately goes to work, respectfully requisitioning the things he'll need from King Artaxerxes.

And I said to the king, "If it please the king, let letters be given me for the governors of the provinces beyond the River, that they may allow me to pass through until I come to Judah, and a letter to Asaph the keeper of the king's forest, that he may give me timber to make beams for the gates of the fortress which is by the temple, for the wall of the city, and for the house to which I will go." And the king granted them to me because the good hand of my God was on me.
(Neh. 2:7–8)

Because the desires of the king's heart were now flowing in the same direction as Nehemiah's, he was pleased to provide what his servant needed. The curtain closes on this incredible scene with Nehemiah bringing us back to the truth of Proverbs 21:1 and the reason for his success—"the good hand of my God was on me."

Nehemiah en Route

In a brief interlude before the final scene of our lesson, Nehemiah narrates us quickly over eight hundred miles with only two highlights.

Encouragement

With the king's letters and escort, Nehemiah had no trouble securing a passageway through the bolted doors of distant provinces.

---

3. The Living Bible (Wheaton, Ill.: Tyndale House Publishers, 1971).

Then I came to the governors of the provinces beyond the River and gave them the king's letters. Now the king had sent with me officers of the army and horsemen. (Neh. 2:9)

Opposition

In verse 10 the beginning threads of a subplot of opposition are seen through a glimpse into the hearts of two antagonists.

And when Sanballat the Horonite and Tobiah the Ammonite official heard about it, it was very displeasing to them that someone had come to seek the welfare of the sons of Israel.

For many people, opposition raises serious doubts about whether we're in God's will. In Nehemiah's case the opposition of those who despised the things of God served as an affirmation that he *was* doing God's will.

Nehemiah in Jerusalem

The denouement—to Nehemiah's four months of fervent praying and waiting, risking his life before Artaxerxes, and his eight-hundred-mile journey through hostile lands—is a view. In the simplest words, Nehemiah leaves us looking upon the city of God— "So I came to Jerusalem" (v. 11a). God's builder has arrived, but no one knows it . . . yet.

In My Homeland Today

All that we have seen and heard today, from King Artaxerxes' dining table across eight hundred miles to the city of Jerusalem, has pointed towards an important truth about good leadership: preparation is essential. Briefly, let's review the highlights of Nehemiah's preparation for a mighty task that are applicable to our being leaders or being workers under difficult bosses.

First, *changing the heart is God's specialty.* No matter how important the person, God is the one who decides the direction a heart will bend. Second, *prayer and waiting go hand in hand.* You haven't really prayed till you've learned to wait, to abandon your own efforts at manipulation and wait on God to work in His timing. Third, *faith is not a synonym for disorder or a substitute for careful planning.* God honors and expects careful thinking and planning from his faithful children. Fourth, *opposition often affirms being in the will of God.* When we are walking in His footsteps we can expect to encounter some Horonites and Ammonites who will oppose us. This may affirm —rather than refute—that we're exactly where we need to be.

![Grapes icon] **Living Insights**   STUDY ONE

Most of us have a *Tyrannosaurus rex* in our lives, someone in authority over us who seems impossible to change. That someone could be a teacher, principal, commanding officer, foreman, director, parent, president, manager . . . you name it.

Do you pray for the Artaxerxes in your life, like Nehemiah did? Or do you pray more like Gwen?

> Dear Lord,
> Please take care of everybody in the whole world Except the landlord.
> I love you
> Gwen
> Age 8
> Indianapolis [4]

If the guileless honesty of this eight-year-old's prayer has cut you to the quick, take a moment to focus on what the following verses teach. Matthew 5:43–48, Luke 6:27–36, and Matthew 18:21–35.

If Gwen's prayer had come from your own heart, what difficult leader's name would replace "the landlord"?

_____

Is there a particular manipulative technique—silent treatment, kill them with kindness, flattery—that you need to replace with prayer for this person?

_____

_____

What is keeping you from turning this person over to God?

_____

_____

4. As quoted in *Dear Lord,* selected by Bill Adler (Nashville, Tenn.: Thomas Nelson Publishers, 1982), n.p. Used by permission.

23

In his commentary on Nehemiah, Alan Redpath says,

> Nehemiah was a man with a burden, who had been
> sent and supplied, a man with vision and vocation.
> Here was a man whose whole attitude was a declara-
> tion of war against things as they were. And as the
> enemy saw his determination to retrieve ground that
> was lost, at once they were aroused to oppose.
>   There is no battle anywhere in the spiritual sense
> until the Christian pitches in. There is no concern in
> the mind of Satan about the church at all until he sees
> a selfless Christian seeking only the glory of God, de-
> termined to challenge the Satanic grip upon men's
> hearts and lives in the name of the Lord. Does your
> service for God cause Satan any worry at all?[5]

Tough question.

Can you think of a specific area in your life that you've held
back from committing to God for fear of opposition?

What do you think the opposition would be like?

What is it that you fear most?

Is there something that you are not willing to trust God to
provide for you?

If you don't commit this area to God, what consequences do you
foresee?

Satan loves to get our focus on the opposition. He delighted
when the whole army of Israel saw only Goliath and not their God.
He smirked when Peter saw the waves instead of the Savior and
began to sink. He probably laughed when the disciples ran at the
sight of the Roman cohort and Pharisees who came to arrest Jesus
at Gethsemane. He may even have *you* running scared because your
focus is on a Sanballat or Tobiah. Take a breather for a moment to
read Hebrews 12:1–3.

This week, will you commit to giving Christ control in your area
of fear? It's going to worry someone. Will it be you or Satan?

---

5. Alan Redpath, *Victorious Christian Service: Studies in the Book of Nehemiah* (Westwood, N.J.: Fleming H. Revell Co., 1958), p. 38.

Chapter 4

MOTIVATION:
THE BASIS OF LEADERSHIP
Nehemiah 2:11–20

Two kindred years. 444 B.C. . . . 1940 A.D. The birth dates of fraternal twins of leadership, born in different centuries to similar crises.

In B.C. Jerusalem, the city walls were in ruins and the gates had been burned. In A.D. London, the walls of homes, businesses, and churches were in ruins and columns of smoke rose to blacken the sky. In Jerusalem, the people were in great distress and reproach from their enemies. In London, a malaise of despair and sorrow weakened the hearts of the people; a ruthless tyrant from Germany was gobbling up all of Europe, and now his jaws were closing on Great Britain.

The leader who rebuilt the walls of Jerusalem was, of course, Nehemiah. The individual who led the British out of Hitler's maelstrom of destruction was Winston Churchill—a man whose speeches were said to be like an army. His words fought their way into the hearts of the people and routed the fear that held them captive. United behind Churchill, the "bulldog of Britain," the British became a tenacious and fierce breed whose jaws the Nazi leviathan underestimated.

As a leader, Churchill faced many of the same challenges as Nehemiah. The Prime Minister's words directed to President Roosevelt—"Give us the tools, and we will finish the job"[1]—remind us of Nehemiah's request to King Artaxerxes—"Give me permission to build, timber to build with, and safe passage past my enemies, and we'll finish the job."

And both did finish the job. They each led their people from near defeat to victory with the same bulldogged determination and ability to motivate that is found in all great leaders.

In our lesson today we will join up with Nehemiah, a one-man army, as he arrives on location at his new jobsite and battlefront—Jerusalem.

1. *Bartlett's Familiar Quotations*, 15th ed., rev. and enl., ed. Emily Morison Beck (Boston, Mass.: Little, Brown and Co., 1980), p. 744.

25

Private Investigation of the Scene

Nehemiah announces his arrival in the first half of verse 11, "So I came to Jerusalem," and then he drops out of sight in the next phrase, "and I was there three days." Three days and not a word. No luncheons with city officials, no press conferences, no guided tours around the wall—only silence.

Silence and Solitude

The reason for Nehemiah's baffling behavior is revealed in verses 12 and 16. Although he avoided the public limelight for three days, we shall see that Nehemiah did meet with an important official—Jehovah. And he was involved in a press conference—one where he took note of what God wanted to do. And he did take a tour of the wall—at night, and without anyone knowing his purpose. After arriving, the first order of business for Nehemiah was to seek silence and solitude.

> And I arose in the night, I and a few men with me. I did not tell anyone what my God was putting into my mind to do for Jerusalem and there was no animal with me except the animal on which I was riding. . . . And the officials did not know where I had gone or what I had done; nor had I as yet told the Jews, the priests, the nobles, and officials, or the rest who did the work. (Neh. 2:12, 16)

Throughout those first three days Nehemiah was pausing to learn. He purposefully avoided the crowds and the mistake of which A. W. Tozer warns:

> May not the inadequacy of much of our spiritual experience be traced back to our habit of skipping through the corridors of the Kingdom like children through the market place, chattering about everything, but pausing to learn the true value of nothing?[2]

In the Scriptures, all great leaders exhibited this same character trait of "pausing to learn." They made a habit out of regularly seeking solitude with God, and not simply at holidays and funerals.

Consider Moses who spent forty years in the silence and solitude of the Midian desert leading only sheep . . . before God used him to lead people. A forty-year pause between the limelight as Pharoah's son and the limelight as Israel's deliverer.

2. A. W. Tozer, *The Divine Conquest* (Camp Hill, Pa.: Christian Publications, 1950), p. 22.

In the New Testament, James remembers that it was in the silence and solitude of prayer, pausing on his knees before the Lord, that Elijah did his greatest work (James 5:17–18).

Paul, the apostle whose voice we hear a good deal of in the New Testament, began it all in silence in a place we know only as Arabia (Gal. 1:17–18). He spent three years there out of the public's eye, being transformed in his heart and mind from a Pharisee to a devoted disciple of Christ.

The one you would least expect to need time alone with God was the One who enjoyed perfect fellowship with Him at all times— Jesus. The Savior lived in constant fellowship with God, even in crowded streets and temples, at marriage feasts and on mountainsides. Yet He seemed to hunger for those special times of intimacy with His Father spent in silence and solitude away from the crowds.[3]

The anvil upon which God molds His leaders is silence and solitude. For it is during these interludes that God forges the qualities, thoughts, and character of a true leader.

Objective Appraisal

When the Battle of Britain began, Churchill could often be found in the midst of the action, "at fighter headquarters, inspecting coast defenses or anti-aircraft batteries, visiting scenes of bomb damage or victims of the 'blitz.' "[4]

Like Churchill, Nehemiah immediately set about inspecting Jerusalem's main defense, the wall, gathering firsthand information as to the damage inflicted by the Babylonian "blitz." He kept the spotlight off his tour of Jerusalem's walls by inspecting them during the silence and solitude of night.

> So I went out at night by the Valley Gate in the direction of the Dragon's Well and on to the Refuse Gate, inspecting the walls of Jerusalem which were broken down and its gates which were consumed by fire. Then I passed on to the Fountain Gate and the King's Pool, but there was no place for my mount to pass. So I went up at night by the ravine and inspected the wall. Then I entered the Valley Gate again and returned. (Neh. 2:13–15)

3. For a deeper look into the need for time alone in silence and solitude, study Matthew 4:1–11; Luke 6:12; Matthew 14:13, 23; Mark 1:35, 6:31; Matthew 26:36–46. In each case note the circumstances that prompted Jesus to seek solitude with the Father throughout His life.

4. *The New Encyclopædia Britannica*, 15th ed., see "Sir Winston Churchill."

The kind of tour Nehemiah made is revealed in the word *inspect* (vv. 13, 15). In Hebrew it means "to look into something very carefully." It's a medical word for probing a wound to see the extent of the laceration or infection of a disease. Nehemiah carefully probed his way around the wall's gaping wounds, gathering facts, organizing plans, preparing to assign tasks, getting ready for a critical challenge that every leader faces—motivating others.

Open Discussion of the Need

With the opening phrase of verse 17, "Then I said to them," Nehemiah leaves the harbor of silence and solitude and launches himself into public notice. Now we will hear the one-man-army speech Nehemiah used to recruit volunteers for the wall.

Presentation

Winston Churchill's first statement as Prime Minister to the House of Commons during World War II was, "I have nothing to offer but blood, toil, tears and sweat."[5] With those words Churchill laid aside all the impedimenta of British protocol and got down to the serious business of committing himself to the people and their most pressing need—protection of their homeland. In Nehemiah's first address as God's leader for rebuilding the wall, he, too, identifies with the people and commits himself to the task of helping to protect their homeland.

> Then I said to them, "You see the bad situation we are in, that Jerusalem is desolate and its gates burned by fire. Come, let us rebuild the wall of Jerusalem that we may no longer be a reproach." (v. 17)

Three times Nehemiah identifies himself with the people, saying "we," "us," and "we." Three times he lays to rest any doubt whether this is just some prattling official from Persia or a brother who genuinely shares their distress and reproach. The people are motivated by Nehemiah's sincere offer of blood, toil, tears, and sweat to rebuild the city's protective wall.

Nehemiah also lays out the hard facts, as Churchill often did. Not to blame or beat the people down, but to fan their smouldering passions into blazing flames.

Finally, it is also clear that Nehemiah makes no effort to motivate the people with external rewards, like new chariots, camp-outs at

5. *Bartlett's Familiar Quotations*, p. 743.

28

the Dead Sea, a section of the wall with their name on it. This kind of motivation has its place, but here Nehemiah scratches the people where their intrinsic motivation itches—"that we may no longer be a reproach." Nehemiah appeals to their desire to assume national prominence again as God's holy people.

Response

Nehemiah concludes with an upbeat report of how God has already begun to bless the work, and the people make their decision.

> And I told them how the hand of my God had been favorable to me, and also about the king's words which he had spoken to me. Then they said, "Let us arise and build." So they put their hands to the good work. (v. 18)

Direct Criticism of the Plan

In an address given on December 30, 1941, over a year after France's occupation, Churchill recalled the mocking the British received over their decision to stand and fight.

> When I warned [the French] that Britain would fight on alone whatever they did, their generals told their prime minister and his divided cabinet, "In three weeks England will have her neck wrung like a chicken." Some chicken; some neck.[6]

No sooner had Nehemiah convinced the Israelites to stand and rebuild than they encountered some of the same kind of ridicule.

> But when Sanballat the Horonite, and Tobiah the Ammonite official, and Geshem the Arab heard it, they mocked us and despised us and said, "What is this thing you are doing? Are you rebelling against the king?" (v. 19)

Answer

The bulldog of Britain once said in defiance to Hitler,

> We will have no truce or parley with you, or the grisly gang who work your wicked will. You do your worst— and we will do our best.[7]

---

6. *Bartlett's Familiar Quotations*, p. 745.

7. *Bartlett's Familiar Quotations*, p. 745.

When the enemies of Israel taunted Nehemiah and his fellow workers, the bulldog of Israel reacted with the same fierce determination.

> So I answered them and said to them, "The God of heaven will give us success; therefore we His servants will arise and build, but you have no portion, right, or memorial in Jerusalem." (v. 20)

"Do your worst, Sanballat, Tobiah, and Geshem—and we will do our best with the help of our God."

Unhindered Focus of the Builder

Nehemiah and Churchill. At times it is difficult to tell these leadership twins apart. When one is described, as in this description of Churchill, you can't help but picture the other.

> A man of iron constitution, inexhaustible energy, and total concentration, he seemed to have been nursing all his faculties so that when the moment came he could lavish them on the salvation of Britain and the values he believed Britain stood for in the world.[8]

Nehemiah devoted his iron constitution and inexhaustible energy to the salvation of Israel and the values Israel stood for in the world. But most importantly, he lavished his total concentration on the Lord in every circumstance. While alone (vv. 11b–12). While before his own (v. 18). While before his enemy (v. 20).

Living Insights STUDY ONE

Most of us are pretty good at dressing up the outside of our lives —perfectly decorated homes, immaculately landscaped yards, polished status-symbol cars, dressed-for-success clothes, sparkling teeth.

But underneath many of our manicured lives are withering souls. The polluting emphasis on empty externals and prayerless activity has produced a smog in our inner world. In unguarded moments of silence and solitude, we can almost feel the grime that covers our real selves.

Is the air of your spiritual life fit to breathe? Or are you feeling choked by the noxious fumes of emptiness and shallowness? Richard

8. *The New Encyclopædia Britannica*, see "Sir Winston Churchill."

Foster, in his book *Celebration of Discipline*, probes the ache in many of our hearts:

> Don't you feel a tug, a yearning to sink down into the silence and solitude of God? Don't you long for something more? Doesn't every breath crave a deeper, fuller exposure to His Presence? It is the Discipline of solitude that will open the door.[9]

Many of our souls long for the fresh, clean air that can only come from exposure to Him. This week, will you set aside some time to come away and just be with Him? Five minutes, ten, half an hour . . . standing, sitting, walking—focused on Him and nothing else? Resist the temptation to hurry through anything, whether you're confessing, praising, thinking through some of Jesus' words, or just being silent with your mind on Him. In the space provided, brainstorm when and where you can find or make some opportunities for silence and solitude.

Places and Times with the Savior

_____   _____

_____   _____

_____   _____

_____   _____

Living Insights

In his first speech as Prime Minister, Winston Churchill committed himself to one task:

> Victory at all costs, victory in spite of all terror, victory however long and hard the road may be; for without victory there is no survival.[10]

Churchill had focus. He led a whole nation to victory because he held on tenaciously—against great odds and hardships—to that one goal.

9. Richard J. Foster, *Celebration of Discipline* (San Francisco, Calif.: Harper and Row, Publishers, 1978), p. 95.

10. *Bartlett's Familiar Quotations*, p. 744.

As Christians we, like Churchill, face a terrible war against a ruthless, soul-thirsty enemy. And the one task we must commit ourselves to is recorded in Hebrews 12:1–2:

> Therefore, since we have so great a cloud of witnesses surrounding us, let us also lay aside every encumbrance, and the sin which so easily entangles us, and let us run with endurance the race that is set before us, fixing our eyes on Jesus, the author and perfecter of faith, who for the joy set before Him endured the cross, despising the shame, and has sat down at the right hand of the throne of God.

We, too, need to set our focus. Not on victory—on *Jesus.* Just as Nehemiah did . . . when he was alone, when he was in public, and when he was criticized. In which of these three areas is it most difficult for you to keep your focus on Christ? Why?

_____

_____

_____

Are you willing to commit to focusing on Christ in this area "at all costs, in spite of all terror, however long and hard the road may be"?

Take a moment to brainstorm some practical ways that you can sharpen your focus on Christ in your weakest area.

Focusing In on Christ

_____

_____

_____

_____

_____

_____

_____

_____

Chapter 5

KNOCKED DOWN, BUT NOT KNOCKED OUT
Nehemiah 4:1–9

J. Oswald Sanders wrote, among other classic works, a book called *Spiritual Leadership*. It's not a very thick book, but it has two great characteristics. One, it's thoroughly biblical, filled with Scripture. And two, it's completely practical. It's realistic. It paints a picture of leadership the way it really is. For example, the fifteenth chapter is titled "The Cost of Leadership"—not "The Glory of Leadership" or "The Recognition of Leadership" but the *cost*.

In that chapter, Sanders lists seven areas where any person, man or woman, will pay a price for being a leader. One of those areas is criticism. Anyone who aspires to leadership must get ready for those needling barbs that are bound to prick along the path. Because they'll be there, no matter how worthy your goals or how noble your intentions. As Sanders says,

> No leader is exempt from criticism, and his humility will nowhere be seen more clearly than in the manner in which he accepts and reacts to it.[1]

Today, as we continue to study the story of Nehemiah, we're going to see our hero come face-to-face with criticism. And not the kind of criticism that merely grumbles and gripes, but the kind that sets up obstacles and opposition. We'll take note of how Nehemiah responds to his critics, and see how his humility comes through the test. But first, let's glance at a New Testament character who is known for his firsthand experience with opposition and listen to what he has to say about it.

Introduction: A New Testament Promise

Of all the New Testament books Paul wrote, 2 Corinthians is the most autobiographical. So it's not surprising that in it we find some honest admissions about the ministry. One of them is in chapter 4: "But we have this treasure in earthen vessels, that the surpassing greatness of the power may be of God and not from

---

1. J. Oswald Sanders, *Spiritual Leadership* (Chicago, Ill.: Moody Press, 1980), p. 147.

33

ourselves" (v. 7). He's admitting his human frailty, the fact that his ministry's power does not come from him, but from the Lord . . . and he goes on to describe what the life of an earthen vessel is like.

> We are afflicted in every way, but not crushed; perplexed, but not despairing; persecuted, but not forsaken; struck down, but not destroyed; always carrying about in the body the dying of Jesus. (vv. 8–10a)

Did you notice that all-inclusive word which begins verse 10? "*Always* carrying about . . ." (emphasis added). The marks of death are constantly on the lives of the people God uses most. And the reason for that is in the last part of verse 10: "that the life of Jesus also may be manifested in our body."

God is not only interested in blessing that humble clay pot. He is interested in using the pot itself as an object lesson in godliness. He doesn't drop abstract truth from the lips of some heavenly angel; He puts the truth in a human life and then places that life in front of an audience, whether it's a Bible study group of five or a mission organization of five thousand. He uses individuals made of cracked, common clay to display—not just hold—the glory of God.

There's a promise implicit in the verses we've just read. It's not the kind we like to hear, but it's one we need to recognize. *Opposition is inevitable.* And yet with the discouragement of that promise comes hope. J. B. Phillips put it in a way that makes you want to stand up and face the fight:

> We are hard-pressed on all sides, but we are never frustrated; we are puzzled, but never in despair. We are persecuted, but are never deserted: we may be knocked down but we are never knocked out![2]

That's our theme for today—knocked down, but not knocked out! Keeping that in mind, let's return to Nehemiah.

Illustration: An Old Testament Example

You'll remember from our study so far that our main character is Nehemiah and that God has given him one main task—rebuilding the wall around Jerusalem. When we left Nehemiah last, he was getting ready to start the project. As we join him now, he's already in the thick of things. But in between, there's a whole chapter of

---

2. J. B. Phillips, The New Testament in Modern English, rev. ed. (New York, N.Y.: Macmillan Publishing Co., 1972).

Scripture we're skipping over, in which Nehemiah appoints various workmen for different parts of the job. This chapter is full of details that only an engineer would appreciate, and since we're not all engineers, let's move past it and on to the part where the action picks up again in chapter 4.

Initial Opposition

So far, the job of rebuilding the wall has gone fairly smoothly. Nehemiah's boss has not only given him time off to oversee the project, but he has also provided some needed materials and even seen to it that Nehemiah had safe passage to Jerusalem. The people of Jerusalem have willingly fallen in with his plans and have been working diligently. As of yet, there have been no major snags.

Until now.

We've had hints before that a man named Sanballat has not been pleased about Nehemiah's plans (see 2:10, 19). But now, with the wall growing daily, his irritation is escalating.

> Now it came about that when Sanballat heard that we were rebuilding the wall, he became furious and very angry and mocked the Jews. And he spoke in the presence of his brothers and the wealthy men of Samaria and said, "What are these feeble Jews doing? Are they going to restore it for themselves? Can they offer sacrifices? Can they finish in a day? Can they revive the stones from the dusty rubble even the burned ones?" Now Tobiah the Ammonite was near him and he said, "Even what they are building—if a fox should jump on it, he would break their stone wall down!" (4:1–3)

For men of power, their dialogue sounds more like sideline junior highers sniggering at another school's winning football team. You would think that a small band of Jews valiantly undertaking such an overwhelming task would inspire respect and applause. But not in these men. The signs of progress and growth and construction just incited them to opposition. Like most habitual critics, they were threatened by the thought of change and saw it as something to be resisted. Also like most critics, they looked at the situation only from the human point of view—they didn't take into consideration that this just might be God's plan.

Did you notice something else about the conversation we just read? It was all one-sided; not an ounce of balanced perspective made its way in. One man's comments egged on similar comments from another. That's because critics always run with other critics. They like to be around people who will reinforce their views.[3] Sanballat runs with Tobiah and another naysayer named Geshem (see 6:1) all the way through this book; they're close friends at least partly through their mutual love of grumbling.

Initial Reaction

Every group—including every church—has its Sanballats and Tobiahs. The issue is not whether they're around, but how to handle them. Let's look at how Nehemiah responds to the criticism.

The natural first reaction is a quick retort. But Nehemiah keeps his cool. His first response is to *talk to God.*

> Hear, O our God, how we are despised! Return their reproach on their own heads and give them up for plunder in a land of captivity. Do not forgive their iniquity and let not their sin be blotted out before Thee, for they have demoralized the builders. (4:4–5)

We can tell from Nehemiah's requests that what he felt like doing was retaliating. But instead of striking back, he spent some therapeutic time on his knees, laying out his concerns before God. Whether he was aware of it or not, he was following the advice of Proverbs 15.

> A gentle answer turns away wrath,
> But a harsh word stirs up anger. . . .
> The heart of the righteous ponders how to answer,
> But the mouth of the wicked pours out evil things.
> (vv. 1, 28)

It takes two to argue; an argument dies on the spot if one person refuses to participate. And it's the words that fly thoughtlessly off our tongues we regret, not the ones that have been pondered in secret before the Lord.

There's a second thing to notice about how Nehemiah responded to Sanballat's criticism—he *stayed at the task.*

> So we built the wall and the whole wall was joined together to half its height, for the people had a mind to work. (Neh. 4:6)

---

3. It's important to note that not all criticism is wrong. Some of it is motivated by genuine concern and is well worth considering. It's up to each leader to learn to listen with discernment and an open heart.

Critics demoralize; leaders encourage. We know from verse 5 that Sanballat's barbs had pricked a hole in the people's enthusiasm, but here they are back at the task, working away with a will. Why? We can only surmise that Nehemiah got off his knees with renewed vigor and that he pumped some of that determination into his workers. "Keep pouring that mortar! Bring on those stones! We're gonna keep goin', and God's gonna help us build this wall to last!"

Intensified Opposition

Nothing riles critics more than having their criticism result in more progress. The sight of those Jews slathering on that mortar and hauling in those stones made Sanballat and his cohorts madder than ever. Instead of backing off, they strengthened their attack.

> Now it came about when Sanballat, Tobiah, the Arabs, the Ammonites, and the Ashdodites heard that the repair of the walls of Jerusalem went on, and that the breaches began to be closed, they were very angry. And all of them conspired together to come and fight against Jerusalem and to cause a disturbance in it. (4:7–8)

Intensified Reaction

Nehemiah's not about to be defeated. Yet for all his determination, he doesn't try to take matters into his own hands. He matches the intensified opposition with intensified prayer, this time bringing his workers with him to the throne.

> But we prayed to our God, and because of them we set up a guard against them day and night. (v. 9)

We can also see from this verse that Nehemiah is practical as well as prudent. He goes to God with his frustration, but he takes action with his common sense. When you know a robber is in the neighborhood, you don't leave your doors unlocked. And when you know your enemy doesn't like your wall, you don't leave it unguarded. As the old saying goes, "Put your trust in God, my boys, and keep your powder dry!"[4]

Application: Some Present-Day Principles

There's not a person reading this, leader or not, who hasn't experienced criticism. It can be demoralizing, discouraging. Or it

---

4. Valentine Blacker, as quoted in *Bartlett's Familiar Quotations*, 15th ed., rev. and enl., ed. Emily Morison Beck (Boston, Mass.: Little, Brown and Co., 1980), p. 444.

can incite us to do or say things we later regret. But what worked in Nehemiah's situation centuries ago can work just as well in ours today. From this one scene in his story, we can learn at least three lessons that will help us keep from getting knocked out every time we get knocked down.

First: *Realize that it is impossible to lead without facing opposition.* Whether you're in the ministry or not, if you lead anybody, you're going to hear some complaints. So don't see it as a sign of failure— recognize it as a part of reality and even of God's plan.

Second: *It is essential that your first response to opposition be prayer.* There's no better place for cooling your heart and getting perspective for your actions than on your knees.

Third: *Prayer may not be all that is necessary if opposition intensifies.* When the heat of the kitchen grows into a blazing fire, you need to pray for God to save you—but you also need to start throwing some water! God's given us the heart to turn to Him, but He's also given us the minds and bodies to take practical action when it's needed.

When it comes right down to it, the carping critic . . . the opponent . . . the pessimist—their barbs are usually hardly worth the worry they cause their leader. But just as a smooth green summer lawn almost always has a few stickers, so every seemingly content congregation or group is hiding a few complainers. Listen to their comments; see if what they have to say has any validity. But if you detect the singsong ring of a lifetime of needless nagging, follow Nehemiah's example. Don't let it rattle your response, and don't let it stop God's plans.

🍇 *Living Insights* STUDY ONE

It's easy to identify with Nehemiah—the person being criticized. However, it's a little harder to realize that we may be the person criticizing—a Sanballat in someone else's life. This may be a good time to take inventory of our speech.

- Throughout this week, each time you catch yourself saying or thinking something critical about someone else, jot it down. This exercise should help reveal what characterizes your speech— whether you're more a criticizing Sanballat or an encouraging Nehemiah.

For further study of the differences between the critic's and the leader's speech, spend some time with the following verses.

Proverbs 10:11	Proverbs 18:21
Proverbs 12:18–19	Ephesians 4:29
Proverbs 15:4	Philippians 4:8
Proverbs 16:24	James 2:19
Proverbs 18:6–8	James 3:1–12

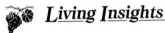 *Living Insights*

Critics usually run in packs . . . like Sanballat and Tobiah, who snarled and snapped at the Jews—"What are these feeble Jews doing?" (Neh. 4:2). And like the Pharisees, who snarled and snapped at Jesus while He hung on the cross—"What is this feeble Jew doing?" (see Luke 23:35).

Whenever we are doing the Father's will, we can always expect the growling and grumbling of exasperated and infuriated enemies. As Jesus warned, "Behold, I send you out as sheep in the midst of wolves; therefore be shrewd as serpents, and innocent as doves. . . . If they have called the head of the house Beelzebul, how much more the members of his household!" (Matt. 10:16, 25b).

If you are being harangued by the scornful howlings of a critic, take some time to think through the following questions.

• How does this person's anger and criticism make you feel?

_____

_____

_____

_____

_____

• How do you react to criticism?

_____

_____

_____

_____

_____

- Why do you think you respond that way?

_____

_____

_____

_____

_____

_____

With Nehemiah's example in mind, try to make a conscious effort this week to respond to opposition first with prayer.

Chapter 6
DISCOURAGEMENT: ITS CAUSE AND CURE
Nehemiah 4:9–23

A mother of eight children came home one day to find her youngest five huddled intently in the middle of the floor. She walked over to see what the center of attraction was and discovered they were playing with five baby skunks. Panic-stricken, she shouted, "Run, children, run!" And run the children did—each clutching one terrified skunk![1]

Can you imagine five kids with skunks, all running in different directions? And the farther each child ran, the louder the mother probably shouted, causing all five to panic and squeeze their skunk . . . and skunks don't like to be squeezed!

All of us have had a problem blow up in our face and end up as a stinking mess. Those situations can knock the wind right out of our confidence and leave us feeling flat and discouraged. And there is nothing quite like dealing with the problem of discouragement when you're in a position of leadership—even if it's only leading five gamy children to a backyard hose.

Nehemiah found this out when he took on a seemingly simple task that turned into a sizable problem. He set out to build a wall, but soon found himself assaulted by the offensive mockery and opposition of some who felt that the Jews' prosperity might put the squeeze on their own.[2] Let's take a closer look at the problem and see what caused the discouragement and how Nehemiah dealt with it.

This lesson is a revised version of "The Problem of Discouragement" from the study guide *You and Your Problems*, coauthored by Lee Hough, from the Bible-teaching ministry of Charles R. Swindoll (Fullerton, Calif.: Insight for Living, 1989).

1. John Haggai, *How to Win Over Worry* (Eugene, Oreg.: Harvest House Publishers, 1987), p. 184.

2. In his commentary on Nehemiah, Dr. Cyril Barber explains why Sanballat and the wealthy men of Samaria opposed Nehemiah's work. "Put bluntly, 'a powerful Jerusalem means a depressed Samaria.' One of the main highways linking the Tigris-Euphrates river valley to the north with Egypt in the south and Philistia to the west, passes through Jerusalem. With Jerusalem once more a well-protected city, its very location will attract trade; and gone will be Samaria's economic supremacy in 'the land beyond the river.'" From *Nehemiah and the Dynamics of Effective Leadership* (Neptune, N.J.: Loizeaux Brothers, 1976), pp. 59–60.

Causes of Discouragement

Since 586 B.C., when the Babylonians conquered the southern kingdom of Judah and took the people into exile, Jerusalem's walls had been in disarray. Now, 142 years later, Judah was beginning to dust herself off after her great spiritual fall and start walking with God again. And God wanted Nehemiah to oversee the task of rebuilding the wall around the city.

As we saw in our last lesson, while Nehemiah's workers were building up Jerusalem's broken walls a little more each day . . . their confidence and faith were being torn down, brick by brick, by the repeated threats and criticisms of their enemies. They were demoralized (Neh. 4:5). And despite Nehemiah's efforts to encourage the people, discouragement finally brought their work to a standstill. Nehemiah 4:10–11 gives us the reasons why.

> Thus in Judah it was said,
> "The strength of the burden bearers is
>   failing,
> Yet there is much rubbish;
> And we ourselves are unable
> To rebuild the wall."
> And our enemies said, "They will not know or see until we come among them, kill them, and put a stop to the work."

Loss of Strength

The very first thing this passage mentions is that the people were burned out physically; the original text says they were "stumbling, tottering, staggering under the load." One of the main reasons for rebuilding the wall was for protection. But in their haste, they had neglected to protect themselves from enemies within—exhaustion. They had started strong, but they were too tired to finish.

Loss of Vision

The Hebrew word for *rubbish* means "dry earth, debris." The people were tired; they had done a lot of work . . . but instead of being encouraged to go on by what they had already accomplished, they saw only the huge task before them and couldn't imagine the wall ever being completed.

Loss of Confidence

The end of verse 10 shows that the erosion of the people's physical reserves and vision had also worn down their confidence. At one time the people "had a mind to work" (see v. 6). Now, their motivation was gone, and in its place was an overwhelming feeling that they could never finish the task.

Loss of Security

The Jews had enemies who didn't want to see them rebuild that wall—and they didn't keep their objections a secret (v. 11). The people had to place each brick while looking over their shoulder, not knowing from moment to moment whether they might be attacked.

Nehemiah's Cure for Discouragement

Nehemiah must have felt somewhat like that mother with the baby skunks—out of control and with a mess on his hands. The troops were wilting with discouragement and his grand idea of rebuilding the wall was crumbling before his eyes. But Nehemiah didn't stand around wringing his hands. Instead, he began putting into action five things which would rebuild the people's confidence.

He Unified the People around the Same Goal

> Then I stationed men in the lowest parts of the space behind the wall, the exposed places, and I stationed the people in families with their swords, spears, and bows. (v. 13)

Nehemiah saw that the basic unit of encouragement, the family, had been broken up by having relatives work at different places on the wall. He also saw that scattering the work was counterproductive. So he reorganized the work and teamed up his people into family units centered around common goals.

He Directed Their Attention to the Lord

> When I saw their fear, I rose and spoke to the nobles, the officials, and the rest of the people: "Do not be afraid of them; remember the Lord who is great and awesome." (v. 14a)

Nehemiah saw his people's fear and knew that he had to get their eyes back on the Lord. Their focus was on the debris and the enemy, and until that changed, there would be no progress.[3]

He Encouraged Them to Maintain a Balance

> And it happened when our enemies heard that it was known to us, and that God had frustrated their

---

3. During times of discouragement, it's important for all of us to refocus our attention on the Lord. We can do this by meditating on His promises, memorizing His Word, and reflecting on His character (see Ps. 46:10).

plan, then all of us returned to the wall, each one to his work. . . . Those who were rebuilding the wall and those who carried burdens took their load with one hand doing the work and the other holding a weapon. (vv. 15, 17)

When we're discouraged, it's easy to get caught in the swings of the pendulum—to see only one view at a time, never the whole picture. Nehemiah probably had some workers who wanted to concentrate on building the protective wall, and others who wanted to grab their spears and go to war. He had to bring the people into a balance of continuing the work while also being prepared to fight.

He Provided a Rallying Point

And I said to the nobles, the officials, and the rest of the people, "The work is great and extensive, and we are separated on the wall far from one another. At whatever place you hear the sound of the trumpet, rally to us there. Our God will fight for us." (vv. 19–20)

First of all, the rallying point involved a place. Nehemiah knew the enemy could attack at any time, in any place. The people needed to know that if one section of the wall was put under siege, the others would rally to their aid and not leave them to fight alone. Second, the rallying point involved a principle. Nehemiah bolstered his people's faith in God by reminding them that He would be fighting alongside them.[4]

He Occupied Them in a Ministry of Service to Others

So we carried on the work with half of them holding spears from dawn until the stars appeared. At that time I also said to the people, "Let each man with his servant spend the night within Jerusalem so that they may be a guard for us by night and a laborer by day." (vv. 21–22)

Lastly, Nehemiah created a protective buddy system. He knew that if the people got involved serving one another that their confidence and morale about the project would increase, and they would be better protected from their enemies.

---

4. Too often, when Christians come under discouragement's attack, they have no friends to recall them to a rallying point. But the idea of drawing together, both for earthly encouragement and to be reminded of the Lord's presence, is woven throughout Scripture. When David was pursued by King Saul, Jonathan was there to encourage and help David. When Elijah was depressed and fleeing from the murderous Queen Jezebel, God sent Elisha to encourage him. We all need someone who will drop what they are doing and come running when we need help.

Our Response Today

Many of us started our Christian walk with confidence and faith —we were like the fellow Tim Hansel describes in *Eating Problems for Breakfast:* "He was the sort of man who would go after Moby Dick with a row boat, a harpoon, and a jar of tartar sauce."[5] But it doesn't take long to start feeling swamped, discouraged, for some of the very same reasons as Nehemiah's crew.

Are you facing the halfway mark in some task in your world? Whether you're halfway through building a wall or half finished with paying off a debt, discouragement may catch you unawares as you lean on your shovel to rest.

Are you overwhelmed by the task left before you? Whether you are knee-deep in crumbled bricks or desk-deep in memos and meetings, the debris of the daily routine can clutter your mind and keep you from seeing the work you've already accomplished.

Has the building up of your faith left you worn out? Have you lost your vision, your confidence? Are you feeling insecure about whether God is really going to help you when those problems attack you from all sides?

Discouragement has a strong, relentless power to pull the focus of our hearts and minds in on ourselves. It can quell our hunger for knowing and trusting in Christ and lead us to trust in our own abilities—but don't let it. Follow Nehemiah's guidelines for encouragement, and resume your task with renewed spirit.

Living Insights STUDY ONE

Since being born into the family of God, many of us have been reared to live in stained-glass houses, emotionally speaking. Ones where we're always happy, things are great, *praise the Lord!* Never sad or discouraged.

In his excellent book *The Marriage Builder,* Dr. Larry Crabb notes that

> Christians are often trained to pretend that they feel joyful and happy when they are really miserable. Because we "shouldn't" feel unhappy, we pretend we

5. Tim Hansel, *Eating Problems for Breakfast* (Dallas, Tex.: Word Publishing, 1988), p. 22.

don't. Yet Hebrews 4:15 teaches that our Great High Priest can sympathize with us when we experience weakness. How wrong it is, then, to hide our emotional weaknesses from Him and to deny ourselves the comfort of noncritical understanding.[6]

Nehemiah, Moses, and David—to name just a few—didn't know anything about living in stained-glass houses. On the contrary, they lived in worlds whose only stain was realism and honesty. There are certainly no stained-glass tones in the feelings they poured out in the following passages. Take a moment to read them.

Nehemiah 1:4–11, 4:4–5

Numbers 11:10–15

Psalm 42

Are you feeling discouraged about something that glass-house etiquette won't allow you to admit? We cannot receive the understanding and help we need from God if we're unwilling to come out of our houses of perfection and admit to being discouraged. In whatever time you can give it right now, write out, pour out, the discouragement that you feel before the Lord. And let these words of our Lord encourage you:

> Let us therefore draw near with confidence to the throne of grace, that we may receive mercy and may find grace to help in time of need. (Heb. 4:16)

_____

_____

_____

_____

_____

_____

_____

_____

6. Larry Crabb, The Marriage Builder (Grand Rapids, Mich.: Zondervan Publishing House, 1982), p. 37.

"He was the sort of man who would go after Moby Dick with a row boat, a harpoon, and a jar of tartar sauce."

For the next few moments, let the following questions guide you in applying some tartar sauce to one of your own discouraging problems.

- What particular area are you feeling most discouraged in?

  _____

- What is feeding that discouragement?

    A lack of strength?

    A lack of vision?

    A lack of confidence?

    A lack of security?

    A lack of something else?

  _____

  _____

- How do you respond to discouragement? Are you depending on someone or something other than God to relieve your discouragement?

  _____

  _____

- What is it that you are expecting God to do before you can stop feeling discouraged?

  _____

  _____

- What is it that you can do—*need* to do—to nourish your faith and hope and to shrivel up your discouragement? For help, read Isaiah 40:28–31; Hebrews 12:1–3; Philippians 4:13, 19; and Psalm 40.

  _____

  _____

  _____

Chapter 7

LOVE, LOANS, AND
MONEY PROBLEMS
Nehemiah 5:1–13

In our last two lessons, we saw Nehemiah do a masterful job at parrying the criticism of his enemies. In today's lesson, however, he faces an even more difficult task—that of allaying the criticism that has arisen among his own people. The productive sounds of a wall being raised up have been replaced with the destructive sounds of people tearing one another down.

The rumbling complaints that we will hear in Nehemiah 5 are not like the familiar ones we heard from outside Israel's walls. These are new sounds of discontent, erupting within the walls of Jerusalem. The issue of money is opening up deep fissures between the people that threaten to crumble any hopes for a rebuilt wall.

The Historical Situation

For many years, the Jews of Nehemiah's time had been gradually returning from exile to live again in Jerusalem. But though they had recovered their freedom, they hadn't recovered from the destruction of their economy by the Babylonians in 606 B.C. Business, trade, farming—everything was either destroyed or disrupted by that catastrophe. It opened a fragile fault line that ran right through the center of Israel's pocketbooks. One that could easily split open if the wrong kind of pressures were put upon it. And those very kinds of pressures were beginning to fracture Israel's families. Their cooperative will was breaking apart, and what we will hear in verses 1–5 is people "faulting" one another in a potentially disastrous upheaval.

Complaints of the People

> Now there was a great outcry of the people and of
> their wives against their Jewish brothers. (Neh. 5:1)

This cacophony of complaining voices is the result of three basic problems. First, there are families that don't have enough to eat.

> For there were those who said, "We, our sons and our
> daughters, are many; therefore let us get grain that we
> may eat and live." (v. 2)

48

Second, people with property are having to mortgage their land to keep up with the cost of living in a spiraling inflation.

> And there were others who said, "We are mortgaging our fields, our vineyards, and our houses that we might get grain because of the famine." (v. 3)

Third, many who have borrowed to pay their expenses are unable to repay their debts. They have left behind years of Babylonian captivity only to become captive to the problem of finances.

> Also there were those who said, "We have borrowed money for the king's tax on our fields and our vineyards. And now our flesh is like the flesh of our brothers, our children like their children. Yet behold, we are forcing our sons and our daughters to be slaves, and some of our daughters are forced into bondage already, and we are helpless because our fields and vineyards belong to others." (vv. 4–5)

Causes of the Problem

In nature, "the slip along a great fault fracture does not all take place at once. Rather there are repeated small slips."[1] Revealed in the complaints of the people are three "slips" that have caused Israel's economy to quake, the people to grumble, and the wall to teeter on the brink of disaster.

The first slip is a famine (v. 3). It is forcing the people to mortgage their properties just to be able to buy food. The second slip is the heavy tax exacted by King Artaxerxes (v. 4). The people are having to borrow money just to keep up with tax payments. The third slip is an implied one—exorbitant interest rates charged by some of the wealthier Jews (v. 5). The problem becomes compounded when a borrower can't repay, because the lender then begins repossessing the land and crops, even taking people's children as slaves in lieu of payment.

The pressure of these three slips is putting an unbearable strain on the people's finances as well as their emotions. Their groanings are the rumblings of a whole society about to break apart. For Nehemiah, there isn't a moment to lose if he's going to avert a disaster.

---

1. *Compton's Pictured Encyclopedia* (Chicago, Ill.: F. E. Compton and Co., 1932), see "Earthquake."

49

The Leader's Reaction

> Then I was very angry when I had heard their
> outcry and these words. (v. 6)

The people's complaints sparked an anger in Nehemiah that, according to the Hebrew word *charah*, "burned down inside him." He was sizzling with anger. Not the compassionate response you'd expect from Nehemiah or any other leader! But sometimes anger is the best response. In this situation, it was both appropriate and effective. To understand why, let's look at Israel's legal guide, the Law of Moses. There we shall see the laws the people were supposed to live by but didn't. Especially those regarding lending and slavery.

Lending

God clearly defined appropriate lending practices for His people in Deuteronomy 23:19–20 (see also Exod. 22:25).

> "You shall not charge interest to your countrymen: interest on money, food, or anything that may be loaned at interest. You may charge interest to a foreigner, but to your countryman you shall not charge interest, so that the Lord your God may bless you in all that you undertake in the land which you are about to enter to possess."

Explicit in this passage are three guidelines for the Jew: It was not wrong to lend money and charge interest to a non-Jew; similarly, it was not wrong to lend money to a fellow Jew. However, it was wrong to charge interest to a fellow Jew.

Slavery

In another section of the Law, Leviticus 25:35–40, are regulations concerning slavery.

> "Now in case a countryman of yours becomes poor and his means with regard to you falter, then you are to sustain him, like a stranger or a sojourner, that he may live with you. Do not take usurious interest from him, but revere your God, that your countryman may live with you. You shall not give him your silver at interest, nor your food for gain. I am the Lord your God, who brought you out of the land of Egypt to give you the land of Canaan and to be your God. And if a countryman of yours becomes so poor with regard to you that he sells himself to you, you shall not subject him to a slave's service. He shall be with you as a hired

man, as if he were a sojourner; he shall serve with you until the year of jubilee."

From this we can see two guidelines: it was acceptable to give one's services to a lender in payment of a debt, but slavery was absolutely prohibited between Jews. And even if a person sold himself to someone as a hired worker, he must be released at Jubilee.[2]

Nehemiah wasn't angry because the people had interrupted the completion of the wall, or because they had possibly made him look bad in front of his enemies. He was angry because the people had knowingly and willfully disobeyed the commands of the Law. God had established those rules and regulations to set the Israelites apart as a witness of Himself. Instead, their willful disobedience was bringing reproaches on the Lord from the pagan world around them.

Nehemiah didn't react by spewing out his anger indiscriminately. Nehemiah 5:7 says he first consulted with himself. He sorted out the issues, and then channeled the flow of his red-hot convictions directly at the causes of the problems.

The Practical Solution

In verses 7–13, Nehemiah relieves the people's financial pressures by skillfully realigning their dealings with the Law of Moses.

Accusations

In verses 7–9, Nehemiah levels three accusations at the nobles and the rulers. First, he indicts them for charging outrageous interest rates to fellow Jews (v. 7). Next, he charges them with allowing permanent slavery of Jewish debtors (v. 8). Finally, he accuses them of losing their distinction in the eyes of the surrounding nations (v. 9). Nehemiah brought their illegal practices before the bar of God's Law, and the accused were convicted on all three counts. It was an airtight case against which there could be no defense, as indicated by their reaction: "They were silent and could not find a word to say" (v. 8b).

---

2. After every forty-nine years, the fiftieth year was to be celebrated as the Jubilee year, the "year of liberty" (Ezek. 46:17). During this year there was to be no sowing or reaping of the land, and "all property . . . which the owner had been obliged to sell through poverty . . . was to revert without payment to its original owner or his lawful heirs. . . . Every Israelite, who through poverty had sold himself to one of his countrymen or to a foreigner settled in the land . . . was to go out free with his children (Lev. 25:29–35, 39). . . . Thus the Jubilee year became one of freedom and grace for all suffering." Merrill F. Unger, *Unger's Bible Dictionary*, 3d ed. (Chicago, Ill.: Moody Press, 1966), p. 352.

Corrections

Like all good leaders, Nehemiah doesn't simply hurl a few rebukes and then walk away. He goes on to propose some constructive changes that can apply even today where wrong has been done.

First, *determine to stop the wrong*—"Please, let us leave off this usury" (v. 10). Second, *make specific plans to correct the wrong immediately, regardless of the sacrifice involved*—"Please, give back to them this very day . . ." (v. 11). Third, *declare your plans for correction in a promise before God* as the nobles and the rulers did before the priests—"So I called the priests and took an oath from them that they would do according to this promise" (v. 12b). Fourth, *realize the seriousness of the vertical promise*—"Thus may God shake out every man from his house and from his possessions who does not fulfill this promise" (v. 13a).

With this final warning, Nehemiah brings his corrections to an interesting conclusion. The tremors that the rulers caused the people are now what they can expect if they fail to fulfill their promise. Only it will not be the ground that shakes them—but the Lord.

In verse 13 the people respond with a resounding "Amen" to Nehemiah's proposals and begin walking on the firm ground of God's economic principles.

The Needed Lessons

Finances still cause tremors today in many people's lives. Marriages, homes, businesses, even churches collapse because of shaky money management. Here are four solid insights from our lesson today that won't buckle under pressure.

First: *God is pleased with the wise handling of our money.* Ron Blue, in his excellent book *Master Your Money,* quotes John MacArthur's revealing statistics:

> Sixteen out of 38 of Christ's parables deal with money; more is said in the New Testament about money than heaven and hell combined; five times more is said about money than prayer; and while there are 500 plus verses on both prayer and faith, there are over 2,000 verses dealing with money and possessions.[3]

3. John MacArthur, as quoted by Ron Blue in *Master Your Money* (Nashville, Tenn.: Thomas Nelson Publishers, 1986), p. 19.

God has left us ample materials in His Word for building solid financial principles into our lives.[4]

Second: *Prolonged personal sin takes a heavy toll on the public work of God.* Technically, the people's finances had nothing to do with the stones and mortar of the construction project. Yet, on the practical side, their sin caused the entire project to grind to a halt.

Third: *Correcting wrong in our lives begins with facing it head-on.* Many of us spend so much time excusing and rationalizing our sin that we drown out the convicting voice of the Spirit of God. Rather than dodging sinful attitudes about our dealings with money, we need to develop a holy disgust for such things and actively root them out.

Fourth: *Correction is often carried out more effectively when we make a public promise.* Like the rulers before the priests, share your promises to change with someone who knows you well. Confide in an intimate friend or a trusted Bible study group, people who can encourage and help solidify your resolve to be more obedient to the Lord with your finances.

Living Insights   STUDY ONE

Most Christians would agree that, according to the Bible, God owns everything. But hidden in that simple statement are some revolutionary implications. Let's take a moment to examine two that Ron Blue points out in his book *Master Your Money.*

> First of all, God has the right to whatever He wants whenever He wants it. It is all His, because an owner has *rights,* and I, as a steward, have only *responsibilities.* . . .
> . . . I literally possess much but own nothing.[5]

Take a moment to read and compare Paul's attitude in Philippians 4:6–8 and 2 Corinthians 6:10 with the ruler's in Matthew 19:16–22. Then ask yourself, "Which attitude mirrors my own?"

———————◆———————

The second implication of God's owning it all is that not only is my giving decision a spiritual decision,

4. For further help in understanding what the Bible teaches about money and possessions, read Ron Blue's *Master Your Money* and *The Debt Squeeze* (Pomona, Calif.: Focus on the Family Publishing, 1989), and Ron and Judy Blue's *Money Matters for Parents and Their Kids* (Nashville, Tenn.: Thomas Nelson Publishers, Oliver Nelson, 1988).

5. Blue, *Master Your Money,* pp. 19–20.

but *every* spending decision is a spiritual decision. There is nothing more spiritual about giving than buying a car, taking a vacation, buying food, paying off debt, paying taxes, and so on. These are all uses of His resources. He owns all that I have.[6]

Do you give the same amount of care and concern to what you spend as to what you give away? Are there any spending areas that you have neglected to bring under His ownership?

◆

We all need to pause periodically and take inventory of our attitudes toward the things God has placed in our care. If you were to imagine the Owner taking something back, would your heart scream, "No, You can't have that, it's *mine!*" On a sheet of paper, identify any possessions you might be attempting to own. Then prayerfully work your way through that list, submitting yourself to His ownership of each item. When you have done this, "you now own nothing and are prepared to be a steward."[7]

Living Insights STUDY TWO

If you were given the assignment of finding an appropriate title for the 1980s, perhaps you would take a principle from our lesson today—"prolonged personal sin takes a heavy toll on the public work of God." It's not very neat or pretty, but neither were the prolonged personal sins of so many public figures, or their devastating effects on the work of God.

Song of Solomon 2:15 says, "Catch . . . the little foxes that are ruining the vineyards." Those "small, innocent sins" that we allow to run unchecked in our lives seldom stay small, and they're never innocent. If not caught early on, those "foxes" wear a path in our conscience till we no longer feel pricked by their presence. These sins become the deadly silent partners in the making of our characters —and they will eventually cause us to lose our distinctiveness as believers and bring a reproach upon the Lord.

Can you think of some personal habits or attitudes that used to bother you but no longer do? You may have a "fox" on your hands that is keeping the fruit of the Spirit from maturing in your life. Put on your hunting cap and start right now clearing out those foxes of prolonged personal sin.

6. Blue, *Master Your Money*, p. 20.
7. Blue, *Master Your Money*, p. 23.

54

Chapter 8

HOW TO HANDLE
A PROMOTION

Nehemiah 5:14–19

What is the greatest adversity that could befall you? Sickness? Financial loss? Family problems? Surprisingly, your worst adversity may be prosperity—a difficult trial dressed in designer sheep's clothing.

Thomas Carlyle, a Scottish essayist and historian, once said, "Adversity is sometimes hard upon a man; but for one man who can stand prosperity, there are a hundred that will stand adversity."[1]

Why? Because few people being promoted up the financial ladder of success are able to maintain their spiritual equilibrium. The dizzying heights of prosperity often lead to pride and then a fall.

Promotion: An Axiom to Remember

One biblical lyricist we know little about is Asaph. However, he did compose twelve psalms that provide some insights into his character. In particular, Psalm 75. From a few telling verses, one thing is clear—Asaph was that one in a hundred who could handle prosperity. First, he records what God says to people about pride, and then he makes his own comment about it.

"'Do not lift up your horn on high,
Do not speak with insolent pride.'"
For not from the east, nor from the west,
Nor from the desert comes exaltation;
But God is the Judge;
He puts down one, and exalts another. (vv. 5–7)

Using the word for *exaltation* that means "promotion, being made great," Asaph, the tunesmith, forged a timeless truth: The promotion of every child of God is because of the Lord's goodness. Promotion doesn't come primarily because a person is in the right place at the right time or because someone is more gifted, educated, or trained than another. Promotion comes because God in His goodness says, "I wish to exalt you at this time."

---

1. *Bartlett's Familiar Quotations*, 15th ed., rev. and enl., ed. Emily Morison Beck (Boston, Mass.: Little, Brown and Co., 1980), p. 474.

And there have been some, though not many, who have kept their balance after being promoted. Like Joseph—who was promoted from the ranks of Egypt's prisoners to the preeminent rank of ruler over Pharoah's household and empire. And Daniel—born in obscurity, then taken to Babylon for schooling, where he graduated as valedictorian. Soon thereafter he was appointed King Nebuchadnezzar's right-hand man. God even promoted Amos, a fig picker, to be His prophet at the temple of Bethel. This rugged country prophet went before the polished priest Amaziah and, with stained hands from smashing figs, announced God's judgment. Three men whose promotions didn't demote God from being Lord in their lives.

But perhaps the best illustration of all is Nehemiah. Even though he was born and raised in captivity, God exalted him to the prominent place of cupbearer to King Artaxerxes. And when Nehemiah voluntarily laid that rank aside to rebuild Jerusalem's wall, God had another promotion for him, as we shall see in our lesson today.

Promotion: An Example to Follow

In the midst of gates being rebuilt, stones replaced, and enemies rebuffed, it became apparent to the people that Nehemiah was an outstanding leader. So they promoted him to the highest office in the land of Judah—governor.

Reaction to the Appointment

> Moreover, from the day that I was appointed to be their governor in the land of Judah, from the twentieth year to the thirty-second year of King Artaxerxes . . . (Neh. 5:14a)

Nehemiah's reaction? He accepted, of course. But nowadays there are not enough Nehemiahs. Strange as it may sound, there seems to be a reluctance on the part of many believers to step into leadership positions. And it's not because we're outnumbered or unqualified. More often than not it's because of the unbiblical idea that to be spiritual you must hide in the shadows. To desire to be in a place of great significance and responsibility is selfish and carnal, we think, so we stay away from promotions. But in saying no to becoming a college professor, university president, business executive, filmmaker, artist, governor, senator, or other leader who fashions and frames the minds of the public, we lose the opportunity to have a Christian influence in strategic positions. The great need today is not just for more leaders in God's church, it's for uncompromising Christians in all levels of leadership, in all levels of society.

The next time God places a promotion in your path, remember Proverbs 29:2.

> When the righteous increase, the people rejoice,
> But when a wicked man rules, people groan.

Response within the Position

No sooner had Nehemiah accepted the appointment as governor than he was hit with the same four major areas of testing hidden in the lining of every promotion.

First are privileges. Every promotion comes equipped with its own special set of privileges, rights, benefits, and special favors. And there are few who can resist using them without abusing them. But not only did Nehemiah not abuse his privileges, he even went a step further.

> For twelve years, neither I nor my kinsmen have eaten
> the governor's food allowance. (Neh. 5:14b)

Although Nehemiah had the right to indulge and enjoy a sumptuous diet built into the governor's budget, he restrained himself—for twelve years. With the people still facing hardship, Nehemiah exercised self-control and refused to presume on the office and the people with his privileges.

In 2 Samuel 15:1–6 is an example of someone who couldn't handle a promotion. When David appointed his beautiful but rebellious son Absalom to a leadership position, Absalom used it to steal the hearts of the people so he could overthrow his own father. Rather than use his position to help shepherd the people, Absalom used his privileges to feed the greedy desires of his own heart.

Nehemiah refused to presume. Absalom refused not to.

Second are policies. Every promotion, unless it's a newly created position, carries with it this next pressure, found in the first eight words in Nehemiah 5:15.

> *But the former governors who were before me* laid burdens
> on the people and took from them bread and wine
> besides forty shekels of silver; even their servants domi-
> neered the people. (emphasis added)

No matter what the position, promotions involve stepping into someone else's shoes—and policies. And that means one of two kinds of pressure: to do what always has been done—maintain—or try something new. In his new job, Nehemiah is faced with three corrupt policies passed on from his predatory predecessors. They had enforced heavy taxes, extorted food and money, and allowed their servants to oppress the people. The political and social scavengers who lived off this corpus of rotted rules surely put pressure on Nehemiah to conform, to look the other way. But Nehemiah scattered them with just five words, "I did not do so" (v. 15).

Hudson Taylor said, "It doesn't matter, really, how great the pressure is, it only matters *where the pressure lies.* See that it never comes *between* you and the Lord—then, the greater the pressure, the more it presses you to His breast."[2]

Not only did Nehemiah avoid taking advantage of the people, he didn't slack off.

> I also applied myself to the work on this wall; we did
> not buy any land, and all my servants were gathered
> there for the work. (v. 16)

What a difference. The former governors pressed the people for all that they could get, while Nehemiah sought only to press closer to the heart of God and give of himself and his servants for the benefit of all.

Next are projects. In every promotion there is a project to be done. Nehemiah's task was to build a wall, and he never lost sight of that goal even though he was a well-known political figure.

> Moreover, there were at my table one hundred and
> fifty Jews and officials, besides those who came to us
> from the nations that were around us. Now that which
> was prepared for each day was one ox and six choice
> sheep, also birds were prepared for me; and once in
> ten days all sorts of wine were furnished in abundance.
> (vv. 17–18)

With over 150 people to feed at his table every day, including officials from surrounding nations, Nehemiah could easily have gotten wrapped up in parties and protocol and forgotten about the wall. Others have, like Solomon. According to the Scriptures, he was the richest man that ever lived. From the revenue of gold alone, recorded in 1 Kings 10, Solomon made twenty million dollars annually, and silver was said to be as common as stones. But Solomon couldn't handle such prosperity. C. Frederick Owen sums it up this way:

> Maddened with the love of show, Solomon swung
> into a feverish career of wastefulness, impropriety, and

2. Hudson Taylor, as quoted by Dr. and Mrs. Howard Taylor in *Hudson Taylor's Spiritual Secret* (Philadelphia, Pa.: China Inland Mission, 1955), p. 107.

oppression. Not satisfied with the necessary buildings and legitimate progress of his past years, he overburdened his people with taxation, enslaved some, and ruthlessly instigated the murder of others.

All Solomon's drinking vessels were of gold, and those of his house were of pure gold. The shields of his mighty men were made of beaten gold, and his great throne was made of ivory and overlaid with the finest gold. . . . Solomon, like many another absolute monarch, drove too fast and traveled too far. . . . The monarch became debauched and effeminate; an egotist and cynic, so satiated with the sensual and material affairs of life that he became skeptical of all good—to him, all became "vanity and vexation of spirit."[3]

Last is people. The meat and potatoes of every leadership position involves dealing with people, serving them, handling their needs, entering into their hurts. Nevertheless, there are still many leaders who don't think twice about running roughshod over everyone to accomplish their objectives. Nehemiah resisted that temptation, and he stayed sensitive to the needs of the people.

Yet for all this I did not demand the governor's food allowance, because the servitude was heavy on this people. (v. 18b)

Nehemiah saw that the people were overburdened and overtaxed. So he adjusted his leadership to lighten their load, which helped to ensure the completion of the project. J. Oswald Sanders in his book, *Spiritual Leadership,* says:

The man who is impatient with weakness will be defective in his leadership. The evidence of our strength lies not in racing ahead, but in a willingness to adapt our stride to the slower pace of our weaker brethren while not forfeiting our lead. If we run too far ahead, we lose our power to influence.[4]

Relationship with the Lord

Dwight D. Eisenhower once said,

In order for a man to be a leader he must have followers. And to have followers, he must have their

---

3. C. Frederick Owen, as quoted by Chuck Swindoll in *Hand Me Another Brick* (Nashville, Tenn.: Thomas Nelson Publishers, 1978), p. 122.

4. J. Oswald Sanders, *Spiritual Leadership,* rev. ed. (Chicago, Ill.: Moody Press, 1980), p. 88.

confidence. Hence the supreme quality for a leader is unquestionable integrity. . . . If a man's associates find him guilty of phoniness, if they find that he lacks forthright integrity, he will fail. His teachings and actions must square with each other.[5]

Nehemiah led with integrity because he always sought to walk before the Lord in integrity, regardless of the promotion or pressure.

> Remember me, O my God, for good, according to all that I have done for this people. (v. 19; see also v. 15)

Being demoted is tough, but surviving a promotion can be even tougher! The next time you're faced with a promotion, step into Nehemiah's sandals and become that one in a hundred who can pass the test of prosperity.

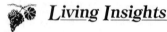 *Living Insights* STUDY ONE

There are plenty of people today trying to push Christians closer to Christ with all kinds of gimmicks, programs, and hoopla. Some even attempt to shove us closer with aggressive, angry words. Others try to thrust us closer with the rough, impersonal hands of loveless knowledge.

There's an undeniable difference between these people and the Christian whose love for the Savior naturally pulls you toward Him. One person focuses on pushing; the other focuses on loving Christ and gently pulls.

Nehemiah was one who pulled.

Imagine for a moment that Nehemiah 5:14–19 is like that popular page from the *Highlights* children's magazine of a picture with things hidden in it. Only this time, you have a word picture to look at. And instead of rabbits and horns, see how many of Nehemiah's "pulling" qualities you can find that came from his focusing on the Lord. For example, the quality of generosity in verse 17.

_____

_____

_____

5. As quoted by Cyril J. Barber in *Nehemiah and the Dynamics of Effective Leadership* (Neptune, N.J.: Loizeaux Brothers, 1976), pp. 88–89.

In your current leadership position, whether you're a mom, dad, president, professor, manager, or minister, which of these traits do you feel is your strongest? Your weakest? Is the focus in your life on pushing others to Christ . . . or gently pulling, through loving Christ?

Living Insights

As governor of Judah, Nehemiah was entitled to some privileges. And it wouldn't have been wrong for Nehemiah to use them, but he didn't—at great cost to himself. What important principle was Nehemiah living out? Read Romans 14:1–15:2 and 1 Corinthians 10:23–33.

What are the reasons Paul gives in these passages for why you might want to give up a privilege or pleasure?

What does Paul say our motivation should be for doing this?

Are there any privileges or pleasures you're entitled to at work, home, or church that may need to be given up or laid aside for a time in order to help others?

Chapter 9

OPERATION INTIMIDATION
Nehemiah 6

Do you remember that hapless Saturday-morning cartoon coyote who was always being squashed, run over, electrocuted, blasted, burnt, buried, and more? This fellow was a genius at erecting elaborate "ACME something-or-other" traps, but it was always his speedy opponent, the roadrunner, who had the last "beep beep." Perhaps no one has tried harder and failed more miserably than Wily Coyote . . . in cartoons, that is.

In real life, Israel's wily enemies—Sanballat, Tobiah, and Geshem —run a close second to their cartoon cousin with their failed attempts to stop Nehemiah from building the wall.

So far in our study, Nehemiah has kept the ravening enemies of Israel at bay as they've tried to run Israel down with mockings and threats. Today, however, Sanballat, Tobiah, and Geshem break off their pursuit of Israel and single out Nehemiah himself. They try to separate him from the people and their project and tear him to pieces. In four separate attacks, Nehemiah's enemies lay out their best traps to try to stop him from speeding Israel's recovery along.

When Did the Attacks Occur?

The attacks on Nehemiah come at a surprising juncture in his life. According to Nehemiah 6:1, the wall is completely rebuilt. Only the gates need to be hung before the celebrations can begin. There's a feeling of euphoria over the accomplishment, and that's when the enemy decides to focus its attacks on Nehemiah.

Why then? Because that's when it would be least expected. As Paul warns in 1 Corinthians 10:12, "Let him who thinks he stands take heed lest he fall." We're much more susceptible to attack when we're intoxicated with success and our spiritual reflexes are limp.[1] Personal attacks are tailor-made for those times when our accomplishments have us walking on air or, as in Nehemiah's case, on top

---

1. For example, when did Bathsheba cross David's gaze? At a time when he had never known defeat on the battlefield and he was at the height of his career as king. When did Potiphar's wife try to tempt Joseph to lie with her? Right after he had been promoted to be Potiphar's assistant. When did Jonah fall into self-pity? Right after the greatest revival in recorded history.

The struggle was political because surrounding cities had become ripe to commerce, instead of Jerusalem.

— Money & power

62

of a wall. The city's main defense is just about ready, but it's *Nehemiah's* defenses that are about to be tested—not Jerusalem's.

What Were the Attacks?

From Nehemiah 6:2 through the end of chapter 6, Nehemiah describes the four different kinds of attacks his enemies tried in order to discourage, frighten, and deter him from finishing the wall.

A Personal Request

The first attack launched on Nehemiah came in the guise of a harmless personal request.

> Sanballat and Geshem sent a message to me, saying,
> "Come, let us meet together at Chephirim in the plain
> of Ono." (v. 2a)

For all their opposition, Nehemiah's enemies have been unable to defeat him. So now, instead of building a wooden horse to get past Nehemiah's defenses, Sanballat and Geshem have carved out a gracious invitation in a letter. Later, hopefully in Ono, they might be able to catch him off guard. It's an appealing peace offering in which the enemy has decorously used the word *together* to suggest that their visit will be as friendly as a high school reunion. And certainly the verdant valley of Ono, only twenty miles away, would be a welcome relief from the rugged stonework in Jerusalem.

But Nehemiah says no. Somewhere behind the magnanimous offer and placating "togetherness," he senses treachery—"but they were planning to harm me" (v. 2b). How did Nehemiah know this? The text doesn't say, but what *is* communicated is that Nehemiah possessed the crucial leadership skill of discernment. Without it, the book of Nehemiah might have ended here—with a funeral in Ono.

Not only did Nehemiah discern their treachery, he also sensed another danger, which he included in his RSVP to the "friendly" summit meeting.

> So I sent messengers to them, saying, "I am doing a
> great work and I cannot come down. Why should the
> work stop while I leave it and come down to you?"
> (v. 3)

There's a great difference between being available as a servant of God and being a puppet of the people. One of the signs of maturity in a leader is the ability to say no. Nehemiah saw the binds awaiting him behind the invitation's benevolence, and he kept himself free from them with a firm *no*. He said it not just once, which is hard enough, but four times (v. 4)!

A Public Letter

After four unsuccessful attempts, Sanballat decides to recarve the letter to give it more the look and feel of a pressure tactic. In addition, he has it delivered via a messenger who would open it for anyone to read along the way. It's highly probable that even Nehemiah knew the contents of the letter before it ever arrived, thanks to the speedy courier service of the grapevine.

> Then Sanballat sent his servant to me in the same manner a fifth time with an open letter in his hand. In it was written, "It is reported among the nations, and Gashmu says, that you and the Jews are planning to rebel; therefore you are rebuilding the wall. And you are to be their king, according to these reports. And you have also appointed prophets to proclaim in Jerusalem concerning you, 'A king is in Judah!' And now it will be reported to the king according to these reports. So come now, let us take counsel together." (vv. 5–7)

When Nehemiah finally did receive his widely publicized mail, stained with the gossipy hands of many eavesdroppers, it basically said two things. First, Sanballat feigned concern over the rumor that Nehemiah's motive for coming to Jerusalem was to lead a revolution. Second, he started a rumor that Nehemiah himself intended to be Judah's new king, in defiance of Artaxerxes. Sanballat then put all his weight into a last spurious concern about the king hearing these reports, hoping to push Nehemiah into agreeing to meet.

Let's step back for a moment and examine the underlying characteristics of this letter—the same ones that are found in all rumors. First, the source is often unknown. Verse 6 says, "It is reported." Who reported it? If it's a rumor, the answer, too, is usually the same—no one knows. Second, rumors are filled with exaggeration and inaccuracy. Sanballat declares that this news is being discussed among "nations," a far cry from the grapevine in and around Jerusalem. Third, rumors lead to personal hurt and misunderstanding. Even though it isn't stated implicitly in these verses, whenever a person's integrity is impugned, it hurts. Rumors are designed for that. Last, rumors are employed by those whose motives are evil: "So come now, let us take counsel together." Sanballat was still eager to arrange for Nehemiah's trip to Ono—one way.

Nehemiah, it seems, cannot escape being impaled on the horns of this rumor. If he refuses to go to Ono, it will be tantamount to saying he is guilty and afraid to let the truth be known. But if he goes to Ono, the work will cease and he'll be walking right into a trap.

The number-one threat to the unity of the body of Christ is not drugs, poor church programs, or even a weak pulpit—it's the tongue. And among those people whose tongues are wagging, several particulars are lacking. First, there is a lack of wisdom. Wise people ask searching questions, such as, "Is this necessary to say?" or "Is this confidential information that I shouldn't be hearing?" The second thing gossipers lack is accurate information. Third, a proper setting is missing. "Will this benefit the person listening or build up the person I'm talking about?" And if the information involves criticism, "Can this person I'm talking to help correct the problem?"[2]

When you run into someone spilling out rumors, what do you do? A loving rebuke is the best response. Plug up the informational leak with a gentle yet firm reproof.

If you're wondering how to respond when the rumor is about you, Nehemiah's way of handling a rumor, beginning in verse 8, is a good example to follow. First, *he calmly denies the charge.*

> Then I sent a message to him saying, "Such things as you are saying have not been done." (v. 8a)

Second, *he puts the blame where it belongs.*

> "But you are inventing them in your own mind." (v. 8b)

Then, in verse 9, *he takes his hurt to God.*

> For all of them were trying to frighten us, thinking "They will become discouraged with the work and it will not be done." But now, O God, strengthen my hands.

Subtle Conspiracy

The next attack from the enemy is perhaps the most ingenious. Having failed at their two previous attempts, Nehemiah's enemies don a saintly look and cloak their evil intentions in pious words.

> And when I entered the house of Shemaiah the son of Delaiah, son of Mehetabel, who was confined at home, he said, "Let us meet together in the house of God, within the temple, and let us close the doors of the temple, for they are coming to kill you, and they are coming to kill you at night." (v. 10)

What better place to catch Nehemiah with his guard down than in the place he is most likely to feel secure—the temple—doing

---

2. Proverbs 6:17–19 lists seven things God hates. Of those seven, three relate to the tongue that sows discord among others.

what gives him his greatest sense of security—praying. But again, Nehemiah's discernment enables him to see the enemy's snare camouflaged beneath the false piety.

> But I said, "Should a man like me flee? And could one such as I go into the temple to save his life? I will not go in." Then I perceived that surely God had not sent him, but he uttered his prophecy against me because Tobiah and Sanballat had hired him. He was hired for this reason, that I might become frightened and act accordingly and sin, so that they might have an evil report in order that they could reproach me. (vv. 11–13)

Threatening Communication

While Sanballat and Geshem are attacking Nehemiah's front line, Tobiah is busy conducting a guerrilla warfare of his own with a barrage of letters.

> Also in those days many letters went from the nobles of Judah to Tobiah, and Tobiah's letters came to them. For many in Judah were bound by oath to him because he was the son-in-law of Shecaniah the son of Arah. . . . Moreover, they were speaking about his good deeds in my presence and reported my words to him. Then Tobiah sent letters to frighten me. (vv. 17–19)

Tobiah had in-laws who would make sure his subversive letters were planted in Nehemiah's presence.

How Did the Attacks Affect the Situation?

Now that we have seen the attacks, let's look at their effects on the leader and the project.

The Leader

Nehemiah stayed on his knees. And because of that, he was able to face the threats without giving in to them or losing sight of his goal to finish the wall.

The Project

Nehemiah matched his enemies' commitment to constantly harass him with his own relentless commitment to work on the wall. And it was finished in record time. "Beep beep."

> So the wall was completed on the twenty-fifth of the month Elul, in fifty-two days. And it came about when all our enemies heard of it and all the nations

surrounding us saw it, they lost their confidence; for they recognized that this work had been accomplished with the help of our God. (vv. 15–16)

Why Is This Important Today?

It is impossible to be in the will of God, to walk by faith, without experiencing direct or subtle attack.[3]

For those times, like Nehemiah's, when you're being pressured to give up, to give in, to quit, Winston Churchill's words to British military students in 1941 provide good advice.

Never give in, never give in, never, never, never, never —in nothing, great or small, large or petty—never give in except to convictions of honor and good sense.[4]

I'm sure Nehemiah would agree.

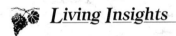 *Living Insights*   STUDY ONE

Intimidation: to frighten or deter with threats.

It's what the disciples felt the night of Jesus' betrayal, when they saw a cohort of the world's greatest power coming to oppose them. And alongside these disciplined, hardened soldiers marched fear, ready to strike the disciples' hearts.

The disciples also saw the temple police and Pharisees. The keepers of the keys to the world they had grown up in now stood ready to cast them out like orphans. The disciples' courage to stand with Jesus fled, and they were shooed away like children.

All of us have had disheartening moments like that in our lives. Gethsemanes where we felt intimidated and ran from identifying with Christ.

How is it that two people can experience the same thing—opposition—and one feels intimidated and runs, while the other

---

3. Of course, not every criticism is ill-meant. At times you may be approached by someone with the right motive—love—who has something to share that you need to hear and act upon. So, the best answer to criticism is not a tough hide, but a teachable spirit.

4. *Bartlett's Familiar Quotations,* 15th ed., rev. and enl., ed. Emily Morison Beck (Boston, Mass.: Little, Brown and Co., 1980), p. 745.

stands his ground, like Nehemiah? What do you think makes the difference?

Knowing God - that He will take care of his own

Living for God

After you have written down your thoughts, spend some time seeking out what the following verses offer in answer to that question, and possibly what they offer for you as you face intimidation.

Matthew 10:24–33, 12:22–30
Romans 12:1–2 — *"Do not be conformed to this world..."*
2 Corinthians 5:1–15
— Philippians 4:6–7
Hebrews 12:1–3
1 Peter 3:13–18 *Keep focus on Jesus* *"fix our eyes"*

Do not be anxious for anything ---

Those who speak maliciously become ashamed

🍇 ## Living Insights   STUDY TWO

Over and over again in this lesson we saw Nehemiah stay out of his enemies' jaws because he exercised discernment. Without that, Nehemiah and Israel's promising future might well have been buried in Ono. Perhaps your desire to follow Christ is constantly thwarted because you lack the ability to discern the enemy's hidden traps. We all need the crucial skill of discernment, for ourselves and also when attempting to lead others. Let's take a few moments to discover Nehemiah's source of discernment—which can also be our own.

How do you cultivate discernment? Read carefully Hebrews 5:12–14, Proverbs 2:1–9, Philippians 1:9–11, Psalm 119:65–72, 97–104, and write your observations below.

Hebrews: Train your mind to dist good from evil; acquaint yourself w/ teaching about righteousness

Proverbs: It is God-given and also the result of a search.

What, besides a deep knowledge of God's Word, is necessary for developing discernment? See Hebrews 5:14 again to check your answer.

dist good from evil "put into practice what you have learned from God's word"

What's it going to cost you to gain discernment?

_____

_____

_____

Are you willing to pay the price?

Proverbs cont'd "store up my commands
within you."
Psalm 119 — God's word makes us wise
wisdom applies knowledge; obey the Word
Hebrews: Paul says "solid food is for
the mature wholey, constant use ..."
We put use what we learn

1 Cor 2 : 6 - 16

Chapter 10
REVIVAL AT WATER GATE
Nehemiah 8

In the late 1970s the African nation of Somalia went without rain for three consecutive years. Relief agencies sprang up in this arid country and established camps where the people could receive aid. In one camp, called Halba, the director took on the task of

> teaching Halba's children to fish in the Juba, where a fast-growing species called *talapia* abounds. Somalis in the camp [had] never tasted fish—hundreds [had] starved to death within sight of a river glutted with them.[1]

Israel faced a similar problem in Nehemiah's day. After seventy consecutive years of captivity, many of Israel's returning exiles had never really tasted God's Word. It was "not a famine for bread or a thirst for water, but rather for hearing the words of the Lord" (Amos 8:11b). They were spiritually starving to death within sight of a rebuilt temple well-stocked with the Law of Moses.

In our study today we will see a revival begin to sprout as the Law of Moses rains down upon the people's parched hearts and minds. Ezra, along with several Levites, is going to teach the children of Israel God's Word so they can once again feed their famished souls.

When you mention the word *revival*, many people think of crowded tents, churches, or stadiums with sweaty evangelists preaching to the lost. But actually, revival pertains to believers. It is impossible to "revive" the lost, the spiritually dead; they first need to be made alive through faith in Christ. Revival is for those who are already spiritually alive but have grown faint in their love for the Lord. It is after weakened Christians have been revived through the proclamation of God's Word that you see the second, familiar characteristic of all revivals—the revived going out to share the gospel with those still dead in sin.[2]

In Nehemiah 8, let's look at the feast of God's Word enjoyed by a hungry people . . . and the stirrings of revival.

---

1. Philip Yancey, *Open Windows* (Westchester, Ill.: Crossway Books, 1982), p. 53.

2. J. D. Douglas, gen. ed., *The New International Dictionary*, rev. ed. (Grand Rapids, Mich.: Zondervan Publishing House, 1978), see "Revivalism."

The Setting

Having completed the wall, the people are now well-organized, well-defended, and well-governed (Neh. 7). But their spiritual welfare still languishes from neglect. So they ask Ezra to meet with them in what will prove to be the beginning of a revival.

The Location

Ironically, the people's choice of a meeting place is a square in front of the Water Gate . . . not a name synonymous with revival in America!

> And all the people gathered as one man at the square which was in front of the Water Gate, and they asked Ezra the scribe to bring the book of the law of Moses which the Lord had given to Israel. (8:1)

The People

In verse 2 we're given the guest list of those who gathered for the revival.

> Then Ezra the priest brought the law before the assembly of men, women, and all who could listen with understanding, on the first day of the seventh month.

One of the key figures at this gathering is Ezra, a scribe and priest. As a scribe, Ezra possesses expertise in two areas. First, he is an expert in the realm of legal matters: he acts as both judge and jury when he stands before the people. Second, he is an expert in interpreting the Scriptures. As a priest, he is able to go into the temple and represent the people before God.

The Reason

According to verse 2 the people are voluntarily coming together to have Ezra feed them from the Law of Moses because their hearts are growling hungrily for the bread of heaven.

The Time

Verse 2 also provides us with the time of year that this takes place, "the first day of the seventh month." What's so important about that? For the Jews, it is significant because it marks the beginning of their most sacred month of the year, one in which they will celebrate three important occasions called feasts: the Feast of Trumpets, the Feast of Atonement, and the Feast of Booths. Mouthwatering titles for a spiritually starving people.

The Event: Revival at Water Gate

United States Air Force pilot Howard Rutledge was shot down over North Vietnam, and he spent the rest of the war fighting to survive as a prisoner of war, a captive in a foreign land. Like the Israelites, Rutledge became acutely aware of his spiritual hunger pangs.

> Now the sights and sounds and smells of death were all around me. My hunger for spiritual food soon outdid my hunger for a steak. Now I wanted to know about that part of me that will never die. Now I wanted to talk about God and Christ and the church. But in Heartbreak [the name POWs gave their prison camp] solitary confinement, there was no pastor, no Sunday-school teacher, no Bible, no hymnbook, no community of believers to guide and sustain me.[3]

Perhaps Rutledge's experience can give us a glimpse into the emotion of this moment when Israel, after seventy years of captivity —cut off from knowing the Lord as their forefathers had known Him—gathered together to hear Ezra explain God's Law to them.

There Was Exposition of the Scriptures

Verses 3–8 present one of the clearest examples in the Bible of genuine exposition of the Scriptures. That exposition had three distinct characteristics.

There was reading of the Scriptures. Ezra read to this nation of former POWs the life-giving Word they had so sorely missed.

> And he read from it before the square which was in front of the Water Gate from early morning until midday, in the presence of men and women, those who could understand; and all the people were attentive to the book of the law. And Ezra the scribe stood at a wooden podium which they had made for the purpose. And beside him stood Mattithiah, Shema, Anaiah, Uriah, Hilkiah, and Maaseiah on his right hand; and Pedaiah, Mishael, Malchijah, Hashum, Hashbaddanah, Zechariah, and Meshullam on his left hand. And Ezra opened the book in the sight of all the people for he was standing above all the people; and when he opened it, all the people stood up. (vv. 3–5)

3. Howard and Phyllis Rutledge, *In the Presence of Mine Enemies* (Old Tappan, N.J.: Fleming H. Revell Co., 1973; reprint, Carmel, N.Y.: Guideposts Associates, n.d.), p. 30.

There was praise for the Scriptures. Ezra praised God for what He had revealed to them in His Word.

> Then Ezra blessed the Lord the great God. And all the people answered, "Amen, Amen!" while lifting up their hands; then they bowed low and worshiped the Lord with their faces to the ground. (v. 6)

The Israelites responded in a spontaneous, unguarded expression of praise and gratitude. The kind of thanks that only people who have ever been deprived of their deepest needs know how to give.

There was insight into the Scriptures. There's a beautiful balance in these verses between the emotional and the intellectual. Had the people gorged themselves only on the good feelings that accompanied this day, they would have gone away and immediately felt hungry again. Instead, each Israelite received a large helping of the Word through the teaching ministry of Ezra and the Levites.

> Also Jeshua, Bani, Sherebiah, Jamin, Akkub, Shab-bethai, Hodiah, Maaseiah, Kelita, Azariah, Jozabad, Hanan, Pelaiah, and the Levites, explained the law to the people while the people remained in their place. And they read from the book, from the law of God, translating to give the sense so that they understood the reading. (vv. 7–8)

Even though the Israelites listening that day were Jews by birth, their whole mind-set had been shaped in captivity by a Chaldean culture that trained them to speak Aramaic, not the Hebrew of their fathers. So after Ezra read the Law in Hebrew, the Levites then translated the teaching, giving the in-depth meaning of words and passages so that the people could sink their teeth into the Law's meaning for their lives.

Today, the nutritional value of what is passed off as biblical teaching is often nothing more than gruel. Flippant preparation of God's Word is causing many to slowly starve on the pabulum of watery philosophies and thin, tasteless principles. For the full nutritional value of God's Word to be enjoyed, it must be served up accurately, clearly, and seasoned with practicality.

That day at the Water Gate was like a massive relief program. Ezra came fully supplied with God's Word, which the Levites spoon-fed to the people. And the visible difference was immediate as Israel's spiritual vital signs began a major comeback.

The Mobilization of God's People

One of the first visible signs of revival that day was tears.

Then Nehemiah, who was the governor, and Ezra the priest and scribe, and the Levites who taught the people said to all the people, "This day is holy to the Lord your God; do not mourn or weep." For all the people were weeping when they heard the words of the law. (v. 9)

Why were they crying? Probably because of the guilt they felt over their forefathers' sins that had led them into captivity. Maybe, too, for those years spent in a spiritual wasteland. With the Law of Moses explained, the people not only became reacquainted with their own laws and sacrifices, they were also reintroduced to Jehovah, the holy One of Israel. And in the light of His presence, their own great sin broke their hearts.

Certainly there is nothing wrong with this kind of guilt. But with the help of Nehemiah, Ezra, and the Levites, the people needed to move on from feeling remorse to knowing the joy of God's grace and forgiveness.

Then he said to them, "Go, eat of the fat, drink of the sweet, and send portions to him who has nothing prepared; for this day is holy to our Lord. Do not be grieved, for the joy of the Lord is your strength." So the Levites calmed all the people, saying, "Be still, for the day is holy; do not be grieved." And all the people went away to eat, to drink, to send portions and to celebrate a great festival, because they understood the words which had been made known to them. (vv. 10–12)

It must have been an exhausting day. It started out with hungry people, moved on to full but guilty people, and ended with full, forgiven, and rejoicing people—a revived people.

Practical Lessons for Us Today

Now that all Israel has gone home to celebrate, let's pause before we leave this incredible scene to consider four practical lessons.

First: *No life is complete without the spiritual dimension.* Many of us are like the Israelites with well-organized lives and homes, but we lack a vibrant spiritual life. We feel the pangs of emptiness as Howard Rutledge did; we feel the same aches of a starving Israel.

Second: *No spiritual dimension is complete without scriptural input.* Just as our physical bodies are dependent on food to sustain them, our spiritual lives are dependent on the food supplied by the Scriptures.

Third: *No scriptural input is complete without personal obedience.*
Hearing the truths of Scripture without acting upon them is like
sitting down to a feast without eating any of it. The people of Israel
not only heard the Word of God, they acted upon it. They personally
digested what they heard, allowing God to nourish their hearts.

Fourth: *No personal obedience is complete without great rejoicing.*
Imagine what it must have been like at the end of the first day of
Israel's revival. People drying their tears, gathering children, hugging, singing, rejuvenated with the first, solid spiritual food they've
had in years, heading home for the happiest celebration they've had
in years. All because they were willing to be obedient. Is your personal obedience marked by an attitude of rejoicing?

🍇 *Living Insights*

Today there is a disturbing similarity between our physical and
spiritual eating habits—both are becoming more centered around
fast-food dining as a way of life.

For example, how many of us hurry each week through a calendar
of biblical victuals similar to this:

Sunday: Sunday-school appetizer out of James
A three-course meal from Matthew during worship
Tuesday: Prayer-meeting snack on Philippians
Thursday: Bible-study-group manna-munchies from Exodus
Personal Bible study: Fifteen-minute-a-day nibbles on Acts

With all this food, why aren't some of us being revived spiritually?

There's certainly nothing wrong with the food—it's divine. Perhaps the reason we receive so little from the Scripture, nutritionally,
is because we allow so little time for our hearts and minds to digest
it. By digesting, I mean seeking out understanding, discussing with
others, personalizing the passage, memorizing, and finding applications.

Take a moment to write down the different message topics you
hear regularly each week. Then write out beside each of these how
much time you give for really digesting what you've heard.

Topic	Time Spent	Time Planned

How much time do you think *should* be allotted for each of these? Add this to the Time Planned column.

How are your biblical eating habits? Is a little motherly advice from long ago needed?

"Slow down and chew your food."

Living Insights

In his book *The Trauma of Transparency*, J. Grant Howard points out that

> guilty people never feel totally at ease with their ac-
> cuser. The one who is unclean doesn't feel comfortable
> in the presence of Him who is spotless.[4]

After hearing the Law, which the Lord had given Israel, the people knew they were an unclean nation loved by a holy God, and they wept. But had they remained quilted with guilt, their sorrow would have smothered any hope of revival.

Does guilt over something in the past keep you from celebrating God's forgiveness today?

According to Revelation 12:7–10, who continually accuses people in order to condemn them?

_____

According to Romans 5:1, 8:1, 28–39, and 1 John 1:9, who is willing to forgive?

_____

Who are you going to believe? Would you rather spend your life in continual remorse, or know the joy of coming out from under your guilt, as Israel did, into the light of forgiveness?

---

4. J. Grant Howard, *The Trauma of Transparency* (Portland, Oreg.: Multnomah Press, 1979), p. 29.

Chapter 11

THE FINE ART OF INSIGHT

Nehemiah 8:13–18

The book of Nehemiah could easily be divided into two distinct construction phases. Chapters 1–6 deal with the reconstruction of the wall, and chapters 7–13 deal with the reinstruction of the people. Both needed rebuilding.

In the first six chapters, Nehemiah the builder and governor is the dominant leader. In the last seven chapters, Ezra the scribe and priest is the dominant leader.

Throughout the first six chapters, the people are at work and the major thrust is physical labor. From chapter 7 on, God is at work and the major thrust is spiritual growth. The emphasis now is upon clearing away the rubble of wrong thinking and the old Chaldean patterns of living—and replacing them with God's design for living.

In our last lesson we saw the beginnings of the people's spiritual renovation in a revival at the Water Gate. There they had the Law of Moses read and expounded to them so that "they understood the words which had been made known to them" (Neh. 8:12). Few things are more exciting than having the Bible opened up, clarified, illustrated, and applied, with the result that understanding occurs. The people went home that night with many of the Chaldeans' pagan philosophies already torn down and cleared away in their minds.

But this was just the beginning of the Israelites' efforts to remodel themselves after the Lord. The second day on the job, certain men returned to quarry insights that were more deeply embedded in the Law—helpful truths that could then be built into their lives.

> Then on the second day the heads of fathers' households of all the people, the priests, and the Levites were gathered to Ezra the scribe that they might gain insight into the words of the law. (v. 13)

In Hebrew the word for *insight* means "to be prudent" or wise, shrewd in the management of practical affairs. Webster's defines *insight* as "the power or act of seeing into a situation . . . apprehending the inner nature of things."[1] On the first day of their revival,

---

1. *Webster's Ninth New Collegiate Dictionary,* see "insight."

Israel was given understanding (v. 8). Now they're coming back to dig for insight, to penetrate below the surface of God's Word for discernment.

The Pursuit of Insight

Let's take a moment to examine, in verses 13–15, the five specific things necessary for the mining of that precious mental jewel—insight.

It Takes Time

There's a great difference between learning biblical facts and gaining insight. The former results in *knowledge*, while the latter leads to *wisdom*. The knowledge Israel reaped from that first day of revival whetted their appetite for more. On the second day, a group of excited spiritual leaders set aside time to delve deeper into wisdom's richest vein—God's Word. Unearthing insights doesn't happen instantly. There's no such thing as an unwise person becoming wise overnight. It takes coming back; it takes time.

It Takes People

Another important part of pursuing insight involves learning from the right kind of person. According to verse 13, Ezra was that rare and essential person Israel needed. It was around his feet that they huddled to gather pearls of wisdom. He was a qualified instructor whose certification involved three ongoing tasks.

> For Ezra had set his heart to study the law of the Lord,
> and to practice it, and to teach His statutes and ordinances in Israel. (Ezra 7:10)

For years Ezra had cultivated insight by sowing the Word through study, watering through practice, and sharing the fruits through teaching.

It Takes the Right Attitude

This was no inexperienced group of freshmen who came to hear Ezra that day. They were heads of households, dads, grandfathers, priests, Levites, all leaders in their own realms, many of whom were probably Ezra's age or even older. Yet they did not allow the age factor to close the door on their teachable spirits. They came with open, appreciative, even eager attitudes.

It Takes the Right Source

Ezra wasn't the people's true source of insight. But after so many years of pursuing insight himself, he knew where to lead the people to find it—"they found written in the law" (Neh. 8:14a). For seventy years Israel had been forced to prospect for wisdom down the empty mine shafts of Chaldean culture. Now, finally, they were ready to restake their claim as God's people and earnestly excavate, without any quibbling over authorship or interpretational technique, from the mother lode of insight—God's Word.

It Takes the Right Response

The expectant men of Israel who gathered to search the Scriptures that day were not disappointed. They rediscovered a priceless celebration that many had forgotten belonged to them.

> And they found written in the law how the Lord has commanded through Moses that the sons of Israel should live in booths during the feast of the seventh month.[2] (v. 14)

Then, an immediate public proclamation revealed what was really in the hearts of Israel's leaders—whether they were committed to simply gaining information or committed to changing lives.

> So they proclaimed and circulated a proclamation in all their cities and in Jerusalem, saying, "Go out to the hills, and bring olive branches, and wild olive branches, myrtle branches, palm branches, and branches of other leafy trees, to make booths, as it is written." (v. 15)

The Products of Insight

Israel's insight into the Law brought about three visible results, differences that show up in all our lives when we really study God's Word.

① Personal Effort

The first notable difference is that a person with insight will put forth whatever effort it takes to obey God.

> So the people went out and brought them and made booths for themselves, each on his roof, and in their

2. This celebration, known as the Feast of Booths or Tabernacles, was one of Israel's three major feasts. According to the instructions given in Leviticus 23, "the Israelites were enjoined to live in booths . . . made from branches of palm trees, 'boughs of leafy trees, and willows of the brook' (v. 40), which were woven together. This was to be a reminder of the Lord's care and protection (cf. Ps. 27:5) during their wilderness wanderings (vv. 32–43) and his promise to protect them in the future." *The Eerdmans Bible Dictionary*, rev. ed. (Grand Rapids, Mich.: William B. Eerdmans Publishing Co., 1987), see "Booths, Feast of."

courts, and in the courts of the house of God, and in the square at the Water Gate, and in the square at the Gate of Ephraim. And the entire assembly of those who had returned from the captivity made booths and lived in them. (vv. 16–17a)

Can you imagine the ridicule these grown men and women endured from their enemies? The same enemies who had just been defeated in their efforts to stop Israel from building a strong, sturdy wall were now seeing Israel's oldest and wisest gather sticks and leaves to build huts! No doubt Sanballat and Tobiah were baffled by the people's building habits—and they probably let them know about it too.

In his book *Enjoying Intimacy with God,* J. Oswald Sanders makes this piercing observation:

We are at this moment as close to God as we really choose to be. True, there are times when we would like to know a deeper intimacy, but when it comes to the point, we are not prepared to pay the price involved.[3]

The Jews chose to be close to God. And they paid the price with their efforts to make booths according to God's specifications, even when it may have appeared ridiculous to others.

Willingness to Change

A second visible difference among those who possess insight is a willingness to change.

And the entire assembly of those who had returned from the captivity made booths and lived in them. The sons of Israel had indeed not done so from the days of Joshua the son of Nun to that day. (v. 17a–b)

Not just years, but centuries of disobedience had erased this celebration from Israel's memory. Yet despite the pattern of forgetfulness ingrained in the people's hearts, new insight caused "the entire assembly" to welcome a change that would draw them closer to the Lord.

Great Rejoicing

Last, those who possess insight are adorned with the joy that comes from being obedient—"and there was great rejoicing" (v. 17c).

---

3. J. Oswald Sanders, *Enjoying Intimacy with God* (Chicago, Ill.: Moody Press, 1980), p. 14.

As inexperienced as they were at celebrating this festival in make-shift booths, and uncomfortable or inconvenient as it must have been, nothing could quench the happiness that flowed from hearts at peace in a shelter not made with human hands.

> But let all who take refuge in Thee be glad,
> Let them ever sing for joy;
> And mayest Thou shelter them,
> That those who love Thy name may exult in Thee.
> (Ps. 5:11)

The Preservation of Insight

Like the men and women of Ezra's day, we all need more than just an occasional insight if we're going to make any real spiritual progress. For a moment, put on your miner's hat and see if you can extract from verse 18 two insight-mining procedures that you can still use today.

> And he read from the book of the law of God daily, from the first day to the last day. And they celebrated the feast seven days, and on the eighth day there was a solemn assembly according to the ordinance. (Neh. 8:18)

First, we each need *time in the Scriptures daily.* Clothing yourself with the wisdom of God doesn't come from window-shopping God's Word. You must enter into His storehouse of insights regularly. Ask yourself, "Do I seek insights from the Lord with the same enthusiasm that I seek today's bargains? Do I desire insight with the same intensity that I desire that new dress or sport coat?" And remember this when you come across a fitting insight for your life: God's Word is not to be tailored to your life . . . your life must be measured and tailored to fit His holy garments of truth.

Second, all of us need to *gather in a solemn assembly for a time of worship and celebration.* Proverbs 27:17 says, "Iron sharpens iron, So one man sharpens another." We all need the honing of our understanding of God and His Word that comes from fellowship with other believers.

If you were to glance back over your shoulder at Jerusalem as you leave this study, you might think you were looking at a gold-rush mining town. The gold of insight has been rediscovered in the long-abandoned mine of God's Word. Almost overnight a whole city of makeshift huts has sprung up, filled with hopeful insight seekers ready to dig for more. With leafy boughs, all of Israel staked their claim to be the rightful heirs of this precious spiritual resource.

There has been an air of excitement and anticipation in the city—people who have known only spiritual poverty for most of their lives have finally struck it rich.

Who knows, you might even see a sign or two saying, Insights or Bust! hung by these prospectors who were ready to gamble everything on being obedient to God.

🍇 *Living Insights*   STUDY ONE

Ezra. He was a leader, a priest, and a scribe—a one-man insight-mining company. And as he was sifting insights from God's Word, he was busy applying and sharing them, gaining even more of the wealth held in each nugget he discovered. But let's take a moment to look at what happens when those three phases of mining—study, practice, and teaching—are *not* in balance.

- How would you describe people who spend most of their time studying the Bible, but with little emphasis on practice or teaching? What would characterize their relationship with the Lord? For insight, read John 14:21 and 1 John 5:3. Then compare those verses with James 1:22–25 and 2:14–26.

  a person is justified
  by what he does and not by faith
  alone

- How would you describe people who work hard at being involved in Christian activities but spend little or no time studying the Bible or discussing it with others? What would characterize their relationship with the Lord? For insight, read John 8:31–32, 15:1–10; Revelation 2:1–5; and Psalm 119:1–16.

  walk according to the law
  of the Lord

- How would you describe people who regularly teach the Bible, but who no longer make a serious effort at continued personal study or application of the Word? What would characterize their relationship with the Lord? For insight, read Isaiah 29:13 and Romans 2:21–24. Then compare the person described in those verses to Paul in 1 Thessalonians 2:1–8. _there can truly —_
  focus on God, not
  _me_

  Excellent for understanding
  application of God's word

82

_____

_____

_____

Do you have a tendency to lean toward one of these three phases .
—study, practice, or teaching? If so, which one?

_____

Ten years from now, do you see yourself becoming like any of
the three types of people you described? If so, what needs to be done
now to keep that from happening?

_____

_____

 Living Insights   STUDY TWO

Someone once said, "Sow a thought, reap an act. Sow an act,
reap a habit. Sow a habit, reap your character. Sow your character,
reap your destiny."

All that from one little seed.

With one insight from the Scriptures, Israel sowed a new thought,
began reaping some unusual building materials, reestablished a forgotten habit, built up their character as God's people, and set themselves on the road again to fulfill their destiny as God's representa-
tives to the world.

All that from one insight.

Are you sowing insights from the Scriptures that will blossom
you into His likeness? Or are you neglecting God's seeds of righteousness in favor of planting the seeds of human philosophies and ele-
mentary principles of the world (Col. 2:8)?

Want to know what your spiritual destiny will be?

Check your seeds. Take a moment to examine when, where, and
how much time you spend planting and cultivating the Word of God
each week.

For further motivation for cultivating the right seeds, compare
Psalm 1 with John 15:6.

Chapter 12

FOUR-DIMENSIONAL
PRAYING

Nehemiah 9; 10:29b–31, 39b

In his book *Spiritual Leadership*, J. Oswald Sanders uses a quote from Dean C. J. Vaughn to rattle a skeleton that hangs in many of our closets:

> If I wished to humble anyone, I should question him about his prayers. I know nothing to compare with this topic for its sorrowful self-confessions.[1]

The truth of that statement humbles not only laypeople in pews, but also ministers behind pulpits, leaders behind organizations, professors behind seminaries. Unfortunately, not even podiums, positions, or degrees can confer any guarantees when it comes to an individual's prayer life.

But beyond just rattling bones in prayer closets, Oswald goes on to therapeutically bring out in the open what many of us deal with only in the dark of our own guilt.

> Most of us are plagued with a subtle aversion to praying. We do not naturally delight in drawing near to God. We pay lip service to the delight and potency and value of prayer. We assert that it is an indispensable adjunct of mature spiritual life. We know that it is constantly enjoined and exemplified in the Scriptures. But in spite of all, too often we fail to pray. . . .
> "When I go to prayer," confessed an eminent Christian, "I find my heart so loath to go to God, and when it is with Him, so loath to stay."[2]

This confusing truth pains a great many of us deeply. And it has been shared by most Christians down through the centuries, yet is still one that we go to great lengths to hide from others—even ourselves. We tell ourselves we're just busy, and that if it weren't for this or that we'd probably do a whole lot more praying. But the truth is, when we do have the time—we don't.

---

1. As quoted by J. Oswald Sanders in *Spiritual Leadership*, rev. ed. (Chicago, Ill.: Moody Press, 1980), p. 103.

2. Sanders, *Spiritual Leadership*, pp. 103–104.

Let's try to take some of the rattle out of our skeletons of prayer-lessness by examining Israel's prayer, in Nehemiah 9, to find some personal applications.

General Observations

In our last lesson the long-forgotten Feast of Booths was about to begin. Now it is one day after the end of that memorial celebration. The spirit of revival has already roused the people from their beds for another unforgettable day of spiritual awakening. To sharpen our understanding and appreciation of the prayer we're about to hear, let's pause for a brief overview of three important facts.

First: *This is the longest recorded prayer in the Bible.* It is one that recaps Israel's history, reviewing God's acts of compassion and kindness toward them over the centuries.

Second: *The prayer was uttered in a context of humility and purity.* It was a strange-looking assembly that gathered that morning. From every direction a herd of people clad in scraggly goat's hair, with gaunt faces, empty stomachs, grieving hearts, and dirt-covered heads, came together and raised their voices as one in a fountain of confession.

> Now on the twenty-fourth day of this month the sons of Israel assembled with fasting, in sackcloth, and with dirt upon them. And the descendants of Israel separated themselves from all foreigners, and stood and confessed their sins and the iniquities of their fathers. (vv. 1–2)

Had we been there, none of us would have had any problem hearing or understanding the confessional bleatings of the people. But would you have understood the powerful thoughts and emotions spoken in the dialect of fasting, sackcloth, and dirt-covered heads? Let's take a moment to translate. By fasting, they were declaring that their hunger for knowing God was more pressing than the need to satisfy any physical hunger. With their loose-fitting garments of coarse goat's hair, or sackcloth, they were expressing a profound sense of mourning, grief, or humiliation because of their sin. By throwing dust or ashes on their heads, the people were symbolically identifying with death, uttering a feeling of the lowest depths.

The Israelites gathered that day with a strong commitment to purge themselves of the leaven of sin in their assembly as well as in their hearts. The first was achieved by separating themselves from all other non-Israelites. And the second came about through earnest personal confession poured out over several hours.

Third: *The prayer reached in four directions.* To help us follow the Israelites' gaze in a prayer that spans history from creation to their present day, here are four guideposts. First, in verses 5–6, the people look up in adoration and praise. Second, in verses 7–31, the focus is on looking back with thanksgiving on all that God has done in their past. Third, in verses 32–37, the people look at their present situation and make a request. And finally, in verse 38, the prayer is concluded with a look ahead.

Specific Examination

With that broad overview packed away in our mental suitcase, let's board Israel's train of thought in verse 5 for a brief excursion across the wide terrain of a faith-inspiring prayer. First stop—praise.

Looking Up: Adoration and Praise

"All aboooard!" Beginning with the single word "Arise," the Levitical conductors signal the people's departure from confession into the heavenly frontiers of praise.

> Then the Levites, Jeshua, Kadmiel, Bani, Hashab-
> neiah, Sherebiah, Hodiah, Shebaniah, and Pethahiah,
> said, "Arise, bless the Lord your God forever and ever!
> O may Thy glorious name be blessed
> And exalted above all blessing and praise!
> "Thou alone art the Lord.
> Thou hast made the heavens,
> The heaven of heavens with all their host,
> The earth and all that is on it,
> The seas and all that is in them.
> Thou dost give life to all of them
> And the heavenly host bows down before Thee.
> (vv. 5–6)

Already we have passed several points of praise. Did you see them? They praised the name of God, which to them was synonymous with the resplendent glory of His being. They praised Him for His exalted position settled on high above mountains. Moving along, they caught sight of the grandeur of His peerless sovereignty and praised Him for His matchless creation, which daily heralds His omnipotence, faithfulness, mercy, and love.

Up ahead now we see one of the important junctions in the prayer. Starting in verse 7, we will begin wending our way through Israel's past. Next stop—reflection and thanksgiving.

Looking Back: Reflection and Thanksgiving

In the lengthiest section between stops in the prayer, verses 7–31, Israel takes a whirlwind tour of their past. Their reflections carefully retrace the moral and physical wanderings of their fore-fathers, beginning with Abram.

Passing through the nascent landscape of Genesis, in verses 7–8, Israel remembers their own beginnings in Abram as well as God's faithfulness. In verses 9–12, we discover the spectacular signs-and-wonders landscape of Exodus, with the reminder of Israel's captivity under Pharaoh and then God's deliverance. Journeying on, verses 13–15 bring us to the border between Exodus and the meticulously cultivated legal soil of Leviticus. Both remind Israel of Mount Sinai and the laws governing Jewish life that were given there. Crossing over into verses 19–21, a panoramic view of wilderness wanderings unfolds in a review stretching from Exodus through Deuteronomy. Then, suddenly, the land of milk and honey appears on the horizon with a brief jaunt through Joshua in verses 22–25. From there, the people pass through the tall peaks and valleys of Judges, remembering the ups and downs of their ancestors' obedience. Finally, we exhaust the itinerary of this section with a brief look, in verses 30–31, at the bloody landscape of disobedience in Samuel, Kings, and Chronicles.

Three sights mar this travelogue—vistas of past failures, which include arrogance, idolatry, and rebellion, found in verses 16–18 and 26. Yet even behind these dismal scenes, Israel could always see a gracious and compassionate God willing to forgive, and that was the most beautiful sight of all . . . one that moved the people from reflection to thanksgiving.

Looking Around: Petition and Confession

In this next section, verses 32–37, the Israelites' prayer switches time-tracks from the past to the present. The people focus again on confession, freely admitting that it is because of their sin that they are facing hardship (vv. 34–35). And in an impassioned plea, they ask the Lord to enter into the pain of living in their own land under the yoke of another nation.

> "Now therefore, our God, the great, the mighty, and
> the awesome God, who dost keep covenant and
> lovingkindness,
> Do not let all the hardship seem insignificant before
> Thee. . . .
> Behold, we are slaves today,
> And as to the land which Thou didst give to our fathers
> to eat of its fruit and its bounty,

Behold, we are slaves on it.
And its abundant produce is for the kings
Whom Thou hast set over us because of our sins;
They also rule over our bodies
And over our cattle as they please,
So we are in great distress." (vv. 32a, 36–37)

Finally, in verse 38, the prayer reaches its final destination. Last stop—commitment.

Looking Ahead: Direction and Commitment

The purpose behind the Israelites' prayer was not simply to provide a spiritual sight-seeing tour. Rather, it was a prayer bound for a solemn agreement between the people and Jehovah.

"Now because of all this
We are making an agreement in writing;
And on the sealed document are the names of our
    leaders, our Levites and our priests." (v. 38)

Chapter 10 records the names, one by one, of those who stepped up that day and signed on the dotted line of the covenant. The specific provisions of the agreement are also recorded in this same chapter. The people agreed to

walk in God's law, which was given through Moses, God's servant, and to keep and to observe all the commandments of God our Lord, and His ordinances and His statutes; and that we will not give our daughters to the peoples of the land or take their daughters for our sons. As for the peoples of the land who bring wares or any grain on the sabbath day to sell, we will not buy from them on the sabbath or a holy day; and we will forego the crops the seventh year and the exaction of every debt. . . . we will not neglect the house of our God." (vv. 29b–31, 39b)

If you were to sum up what the people were committing themselves to that day, you could easily explain it with one word—*obedience*.

The Israelites had begun to look to their future. They had remembered the terrible consequences of disobedience suffered by their forefathers and realized that this would be not only their past, but their future as well, if a change wasn't made.

Personal Application

Whenever we return from a trip we carry back with us memories in the form of ticket stubs, photographs, and souvenirs picked up

along the way. From our journey today, I hope you will carry back
with you the four dimensions in Israel's prayer:

1. Praising—looking up
2. Reflecting—looking back
3. Petitioning—looking at the situation
4. Commitment—looking ahead

🍇 *Living Insights* STUDY ONE

In the preface to his book, *The Knowledge of the Holy,* A. W.
Tozer explains that he felt compelled to write because of a

> condition which has existed in the Church for some
> years and is steadily growing worse. I refer to the loss
> of the concept of majesty from the popular religious
> mind. The Church has surrendered her once lofty con-
> cept of God and has substituted for it one so low, so
> ignoble, as to be utterly unworthy of thinking, wor-
> shiping men. . . .
>
> . . . the God we must see is not the utilitarian
> God who is having such a run of popularity today,
> whose chief claim to men's attention is His ability to
> bring them success in their various undertakings and
> who for that reason is being cajoled and flattered by
> everyone who wants a favor. The God we must learn
> to know is the Majesty in the heavens, God the Father
> Almighty, Maker of heaven and earth, the only wise
> God our Saviour.[3]

Many of us are feeling impoverished in our understanding of God
because we've lost one of our most valuable spiritual possessions—a
majestic concept of God. But it *can* be recovered.

In the Scriptures God is known by many names. And with each
name something different about His character is revealed. Take a
few minutes, an hour, a week, a lifetime, and cultivate a deeper,
richer understanding of God with a meditation on His names.

Listed below are some verses that use the two most common
names for God, Jehovah and Elohim, in partnership with a descrip-
tive phrase. Look up each reference and then meditatively write out,
beneath each one, all the thoughts about His character that this

---

3. A. W. Tozer, *The Knowledge of the Holy* (San Francisco, Calif.: Harper and Row,
Publishers, 1961), pp. vii, 114.

name reveals to you. Next, jot down when you might have felt or seen this particular trait of God most clearly in your own life.

The Lord Will Provide: Jehovah-Jireh
Genesis 22:14

_____

_____

_____

_____

The Lord Our Peace: Jehovah-Shalom
Judges 6:24

_____

_____

_____

_____

The Lord Our Righteousness: Jehovah-Tsidkenu
Jeremiah 23:6

_____

_____

_____

_____

For further study, you might enjoy studying some other names of God.

> The Lord That Heals: Jehovah-Rapha (Exod. 15:26)
> The Lord Our Banner: Jehovah-Nissi (Exod. 17:15)
> The Lord That Sanctifies: Jehovah-Qadash (Lev. 20:8)
> The Lord Is There: Jehovah-Shammah (Ezek. 48:35)
> The Lord of Hosts: Jehovah-Sabaoth (1 Sam. 1:3)
> The Lord My Shepherd: Jehovah-Raah (Ps. 23:1)
> Most High God: El-Elyon (Gen. 14:18)
> Everlasting God: El-Olam (Gen. 21:33)
> Almighty God: El-Shaddai (Gen. 17:1)

You might also enjoy reading A. W. Tozer's _The Knowledge of the Holy_ (San Francisco, Calif.: Harper and Row, Publishers, 1961) or J. I Packer's _Knowing God_ (Downers Grove, Ill.: InterVarsity Press, 1973).

Praise and thanksgiving for who God is, and the wonderful things He has done, was an essential part of Israel's prayer and revival. Today, praise and thanksgiving on the part of many believers seems almost nonexistent, except for the perfunctory thanks given before banquets, athletic events, and holiday dinners.

Are you losing your awe of God and awareness of His presence because of a lack of praise and thanksgiving? Set apart some time now to praise and thank Him, using the list of insights gained from meditating on the names of God in the Living Insights section on the previous page.

Chapter 13

PUTTING FIRST THINGS FIRST

Nehemiah 10:28–39

In an interview several years ago, a very successful industrialist was asked what, in all his dealings with people, was the most difficult thing to get them to do. After a brief reflection he answered that he would name two things, in the order of their importance. The first and most difficult was getting people to think before they act. The second was maintaining proper priorities, doing things in the order of their importance. Another industrialist, Henry Ford, once said, "Thinking is the hardest work there is, which is the probable reason why so few engage in it."[1]

The book of Nehemiah provides a powerful testimony to the importance of preceding any action with careful thought. For example, when Nehemiah heard that the wall was still down and the people were in distress, he didn't grab a trowel and head for Jerusalem. First, he spent four months poring over this problem with the brick and mortar of thought and prayer. When opposition came, he controlled his knee-jerk inclination to retaliate and took time to plan the best way to respond. And Israel, when it came to reorganizing their government according to God's commands, didn't plunge into the task with blind zeal. They first spent time regaining their spiritual vision through thinking and meditating on God's Law.

In our lesson today, the people of Jerusalem want to establish some priorities, to put first things first. And again this is preceded by some in-depth thinking about the greatness of God, His gracious dealings in their past, their needs, and how the pattern of their long history of failure might be changed (chap. 9). All of this leads to a decision—a right decision to reverse the wrong priorities that have come from foolish thinking. With the last verse in chapter 9, the people's focus pivots from meditative prayer to the making of an agreement based on new priorities. But before we look at those new priorities, let's look at the document itself.

---

1. As quoted by Susan Schaeffer Macaulay in *How to Be Your Own Selfish Pig* (Elgin, Ill.: David C. Cook Publishing Co., Chariot Books, 1982), p. 15.

The Document of Promise

On July 2, 1776, a group of early American colonists known as the Continental Congress voted to ratify the contents of one of our nation's most cherished documents—the Declaration of Independence. In our lesson today, Israel will be conducting a continental congress of their own as the nation's leaders step up to sign their names to one of their most important documents—a "declaration of dependence on God."

What Was It?

As we saw in our last lesson, Nehemiah 9:38 describes the document as an "agreement in writing." It was an official contract between the people and the Lord to reestablish new priorities built on His laws. Nehemiah 10:29 uses two other words to describe the document: *curse* and *oath*. Inherent in the word for *curse* is the idea of coming into an oath with God that, if broken, allows the consequences of a curse. The word *oath* is a vivid term that actually means "to seven oneself." In that day, the Hebrews didn't seal a contract or an oath with a mere handshake or a signature on a piece of papyrus. Instead, they did seven things related to their oath as a way of binding themselves to the keeping of their promise.[2]

Even though we're not told what seven things the people did, Ecclesiastes 5:2–5 leaves little doubt that the people took seriously the making of vows to God.

> Do not be hasty in word or impulsive in thought to bring up a matter in the presence of God. For God is in heaven and you are on the earth; therefore let your words be few. For the dream comes through much effort, and the voice of a fool through many words. When you make a vow to God, do not be late in paying it, for He takes no delight in fools. Pay what you vow! It is better that you should not vow than that you should vow and not pay.

Who Signed It?

The signers of this declaration of dependence on God numbered eighty-four in all. Following Nehemiah's signature were the names of twenty-two priests (Neh. 10:1–8), seventeen Levites (vv. 9–13), and forty-four leaders of the people (vv. 14–27).

---

2. For example, Genesis 21 records Abraham's promise to King Abimelech. Abraham signed his name on the dotted line of this agreement by giving the king seven ewe lambs. These lambs were living reminders of the oath that was made.

When the United States' Declaration of Independence was signed, it did not establish the country's independence; "it merely stated an intention and the cause for action. It [had to] be converted into fact by force."[3] In the same way, the good intentions contained in Israel's document didn't establish their dependence. Those intentions needed to be converted into reality through obedience. And according to verse 28, the people who were committing themselves to this task had two things in common.

First, the people physically removed themselves from the pagan influence of foreigners—they "separated themselves from the peoples of the lands to the law of God." And second, they only invited participants who were old enough to understand the contents of the document—"all those who had knowledge and understanding."

Why Was It Important?

Just like America's colonists, Israel needed a rallying point, some unifying formal declaration telling friends and enemies alike of the decision to change their ways. America's Declaration of Independence was the birth certificate of a brand new nation. Israel's declaration of dependence became the birth certificate of a spiritually reborn nation.

The Promises in the Document

Now let's look inside the document at the promises, general and specific, to which the people committed themselves.

Generally

Israel knew what many Americans have forgotten—that life, liberty, and the pursuit of happiness all rest on our relationship with God. And so the general theme behind Israel's document is one of obedience to His written Word.

> Now the rest of the people . . . are joining with their kinsmen, their nobles, and are taking on themselves a curse and an oath to walk in God's law, which was given through Moses, God's servant, and to keep and to observe all the commandments of God our Lord, and His ordinances and His statutes. (vv. 28–29)

The Jews' promise of obedience was, at the same time, an official declaration of secession—they were separating themselves from a

---

3. *Compton's Pictured Encyclopedia* (Chicago, Ill.: F. E. Compton and Co., 1932), see "Declaration of Independence."

world that followed the whims of the latest philosophies and pagan religions. To do this, Israel had to resist the powerful urgings psychologists call the "herd instinct"—the pressure to conform with our peers in order to avoid ridicule and rejection.

How powerful is the herd instinct? Dr. Ruth Berenda shows us in the following study.

> She and her associates brought ten adolescents into a room and told them that they were going to study their perception (how well they could see). To test this ability, they planned to hold up cards on which three lines were drawn. The lines were marked A, B, and C and were of three different lengths. . . . Line A was the longest on some cards, while lines B or C were longer on others. As the cards were held before the class, the researcher would point to A, B, and C consecutively, asking the students to raise their hands when the pointer was directed at the longest line. . . .
>
> What one student didn't know, however, is that the other nine had been brought in early and told to vote for the second longest line. The purpose was to test the effect of group pressure on that lonely individual.
>
> The experiment began with nine teen-agers voting for the wrong line. The stooge would typically glance around, frown in confusion, and slip his hand up with the group. The instructions were repeated and the next card was raised. Time after time, the self-conscious stooge would sit there saying a short line is longer than a long line, simply because he lacked the courage to challenge the group. This remarkable conformity occurred in about seventy-five percent of the cases, and was true of small children and high-school students as well.[4]

In a far more difficult position than that lone student in the study, Israel faced voting against a classroom of nations. While the whole world was raising their hands for the wrong answers about life, Israel was willing to stand alone in voting for the right answer—obeying the Lord.

---

4. Based on a study by Ruth W. Berenda, as cited by James Dobson in *Hide or Seek* (Old Tappan, N.J.: Fleming H. Revell Co., 1974), pp. 116–17.

Specifically

Following their general declaration of allegiance to the Lord, Israel then got specific about their promise of obedience in three important areas.

The home. The Israelites promised to keep their relationships swept clean of foreign influence.

> We will not give our daughters to the peoples of the land or take their daughters for our sons. (v. 30)

From experience, Israel knew that the Achilles' heel, which had exposed them to defeat many times before, was their intermixing in marriage with people of pagan lands. The exchange of sons and daughters had also brought the exchange of religions, eventually diluting the fidelity of Israel's faith in Jehovah.

One painful memory that may have prompted Israel's promise is in Judges 3. The Jews had been led out of bondage from Egypt into the promised land of Canaan. Just prior to entering, Moses told the people that this land flowing with milk and honey had a forbidden fruit. No Israelite was to pick a wife for himself from among the pagan nations or give his daughter away to a foreigner. But the new residents of that Edenic land couldn't resist tasting the fruit, and their disobedience plunged the nation back into bondage.

> And the sons of Israel lived among the Canaanites, the Hittites, the Amorites, the Perizzites, the Hivites, and the Jebusites; and they took their daughters for themselves as wives, and gave their own daughters to their sons, and served their gods. And the sons of Israel did what was evil in the sight of the Lord, and forgot the Lord their God, and served the Baals and the Asheroth. Then the anger of the Lord was kindled against Israel, so that He sold them into the hands of Cushan-rishathaim king of Mesopotamia; and the sons of Israel served Cushan-rishathaim eight years. (vv. 5–8)

The society. With the second promise, Israel extended their obedience from their homes into the marketplace.

> As for the peoples of the land who bring wares or any grain on the sabbath day to sell, we will not buy from them on the sabbath or a holy day; and we will forego the crops the seventh year and the exaction of every debt. (Neh. 10:31)

Distinctiveness was being restored to the weekly and yearly calendars that governed Israel's life. According to Keith Miller, this kind of visible difference is sorely missing in many Christians' lives today.

> It has never ceased to amaze me that we Christians have developed a kind of selective vision which allows us to be deeply and sincerely involved in worship and church activities and yet almost totally pagan in the day in, day out guts of our business lives . . . and never realize it.[5]

The place of worship. In verses 32–39, the house of God, which is Israel's place of worship, is mentioned nine times. Regarding worship, verse 39 sums up the promises of the people in these words: "Thus we will not neglect the house of our God."

At this time in Israel's history the temple was literally the dwelling place of God. Today, however, the presence of God is not kept in a building made with human hands. In 1 Corinthians 3:16, Paul gives us God's new address.

> Do you not know that you are a temple of God, and that the Spirit of God dwells in you?

Wherever we go, whatever we say, whatever we think or do, we as believers always carry with us the presence of the Lord in the temple of our bodies.

Conclusions Drawn from the Document's Example

Our own lives can be living documents of obedience to our Lord, but there are three principles from our lesson that we need to heed.

First: *Serious thought precedes any significant change.* One individual who devoted a lot of time to thinking and hammering out priorities was Henry David Thoreau. In his philosophical narrative, *Walden,* he quips, "As if you could kill time without injuring eternity."[6] You cannot waste time dabbling in shallow thinking and careless priorities without diminishing what you will be and do in the future.

Second: *Written plans confirm right priorities.* Most of us are not used to writing our priorities down on paper. Typically they are kept

---

5. Keith Miller, *The Taste of New Wine* (Waco, Tex.: Word Books, 1965), p. 79.

6. Henry David Thoreau, *Thoreau: Walden and Other Writings,* ed. Joseph Wood Krutch (New York, N.Y.: Bantam Books, 1971), p. 111.

like children's toys in a mental chest full of ideas all jumbled together. Disentangling them from the frivolous, the unrelated, and the outdated requires writing them down, straightening them out on paper. Otherwise, all those impressive priorities we carry around in our heads and occasionally discuss with others will simply remain mental toys, and never become life-changing catalysts.

Third: *Loss of distinction and conformity to the world go hand in hand.* Apart from your attendance at Bible studies and church, can anyone "read" you to understand something about the distinctiveness of Christianity? Look at your home, your work, your relationships, and ask yourself, "Am I really any different from the world?"

🍇 *Living Insights* STUDY ONE

Remember when you were little, how you used to sit within inches of the TV set watching your favorite Westerns? There were shoot-outs and saloons, and you could always count on witnessing a stampede or two.

The Bible doesn't have any shoot-outs or saloons, but it does have more than a few stampedes racing across its pages—the kind triggered in people's hearts and minds by the "herd instinct," or the pressure to conform. Let's look at a few biblical characters who got swept away by some wild-eyed stampeding herds.

Remember the night Simon Peter's faith got trampled by the herd instinct? For help, read John 18:1–27.

Remember the early morning when Pilate's courage got spooked and bolted? For help, read John 18:28–~~19:16.~~ *(was it Courage?)*

Remember when Abraham's faith got the jitters and broke into a run? For help, read Genesis 12:1–20, 20:1–11.

Take a moment to look at each of these men's situations, and see how many different pressures there were, both from within and from without, that caused them to panic and run. For example: Simon Peter felt the pressure to conform for fear of rejection. What else might he have been feeling?

Simon Peter: *Fear of death - crucifixion*

_____

_____

What do Bible scholars know/believe about Pilate?

Pilate: _____

_____

_____

Abraham: *persecution or death* _____

_____

_____

Have you been in any stampedes lately? Is there a particular person or place that pressures you more than any other to conform to the world's standards instead of Christ's?

_____

Of the pressures you listed for Simon Peter, Pilate, and Abraham, which are the most difficult for you?

_____

_____

_____

🍇 *Living Insights*   STUDY TWO

Satan is an experienced hand when it comes to manipulating people with pressures to conform. But not even Satan is successful every time he throws a loop. We know that he rustled Peter's faith away from him, but only a short time later Jesus gently helped His disciple recover all of it and more. And there have been many others who Satan simply could not corral into rebelling against God. Take a moment and look closely at a few individuals who kept the herd instinct firmly in check. In each case, note the pressures involved and then write out why you think this person was able to resist the pressure to conform.

Shadrach, Meshach, and Abed-nego (Dan. 3): _____

Firm belief in God's deliverance _____

_____

_____

99

Joshua (Num. 13–14): _____

_____

_____

_____

_____

Jesus (Matt. 4:1–11): _Satan tempt_
Jesus in the wilderness
Because Jesus is God

_____

_____

Here are a few verses that should add to your understanding of how these people were able to resist the herd instinct—and how you can too. Read Romans 12:2, John 8:31–32, Psalm 119:11, 2 Corinthians 5:16–17, and 1 Corinthians 15:33.

do not conform

Know the Word

Chapter 14

IN HONOR OF THE WILLING UNKNOWNS

Nehemiah 7:1-4; 11

You've probably seen her name and forgotten it a hundred times . . . yet her words you probably know by heart. She's one of God's "willing unknowns." Someone whose life touches others with the brilliance of a sunray, but whose own existence remains in the shadows. Listen to her story:

> One of the greatest evangelistic hymns of all time was written by a woman who knew well the release and peace that comes from confessing one's sins and failures to God. "Just As I Am," a hymn frequently sung at the close of evangelistic meetings, was written by Charlotte Elliott, who at one time had been very bitter with God about the circumstances of her life.
>
> Charlotte was an invalid from her youth and deeply resented the constraints her handicap placed on her activities. In an emotional outburst on one occasion, she expressed those feelings to Dr. Cesar Malan, a minister visiting in her home. He listened and was touched by her distress, but he insisted that her problems should not divert her attention from what she most needed to hear. He challenged her to turn her life over to God, to come to him just as she was, with all her bitterness and anger.
>
> She resented what seemed to be an almost callous attitude on his part, but God spoke to her through him, and she committed her life to the Lord. Each year on the anniversary of that decision, Dr. Malan wrote Charlotte a letter, encouraging her to continue to be strong in the faith. But even as a Christian she had doubts and struggles.
>
> One particularly sore point was her inability to effectively get out and serve the Lord. At times she almost resented her brother's successful preaching and evangelistic ministry. She longed to be used of God herself, but she felt that her health prevented it. Then in 1836, on the fourteenth anniversary of her

conversion, while she was alone in the evening, the forty-seven-year-old Charlotte Elliott wrote her spiritual autobiography in verse. Here, in this prayer of confession, she poured out her feelings to God—feelings that countless individuals have identified with in the generations that followed. The third stanza, perhaps more than the others, described her own pilgrimage:

> Just as I am, tho tossed about
> With many a conflict, many a doubt,
> Fightings and fears within, without,
> O Lamb of God, I come! I come!

Many years later, when reflecting on the impact his sister made in penning this one hymn, the Reverend Henry Venn Elliott said, "In the course of a long ministry I hope I have been permitted to see some fruit of my labors, but I feel far more has been done by a single hymn of my sister's, 'Just As I Am.'"[1]

Charlotte Elliott is only one of the many willing unknowns whose lives have made a difference. Have you ever heard of Athaiah, the son of Uzziah? Or Raamiah or Nahamanni? How about Maaseiah, the son of Baruch? It's doubtful, for they are mentioned only once in the entire Bible, in a long list of unpronounceable names of men whose significance is seldom remembered. Yet they each played a crucial role in the success of Nehemiah's project—reestablishing the city of Jerusalem. And it's their story we're going to read about today.

Historical Background

You may have noticed in our study of the book of Nehemiah that we skipped chapter 7. It wasn't accidental; we were saving it, because it fits best as a backdrop to chapter 11. Let's review what has been happening.

As we come to chapter 7, the wall has just been completed (v. 1a); security has been established (v. 1b); responsibility has been delegated (v. 2); and the daily schedule has been set (v. 3). Everything seems to be running smoothly at last . . . except for one thing.

> Now the city was large and spacious, but the people in it were few and the houses were not built. (v. 4)

How on earth could this be true of a major city like Jerusalem? To understand, you have to remember that this ancient city had not

---

1. Ruth A. Tucker, *Sacred Stories* (Grand Rapids, Mich.: Zondervan Publishing House, Daybreak Books, 1989), p. 10.

had a protective wall around it for a good 160 years—it was open season all year round to their enemies. And on top of that, the rubble and ruin of the city's destruction ninety years before still had not been cleared away; the people had found it easier just to build homes in nearby hamlets. As a result, practically the only people who actually lived inside the city limits were the leaders (see 11:1).

Part of Nehemiah's purpose in restoring the city's wall was to restore the city itself. To a Jew, Zion—Jerusalem—was a place to be honored, the place of God's delight. So once the wall was in place, Nehemiah's next task was to get some people behind it. The people chose a tangible, nondiscriminatory way of deciding who would make the move.

> [They] cast lots to bring one out of ten to live in Jeru-
> salem, the holy city, while nine-tenths remained in
> the other cities. (11:1)

Sounds pretty arbitrary, and it was. But God was obviously at work in the effort to repopulate Jerusalem, because He didn't leave it at that. He also worked in the hearts of some who hadn't been chosen to go.

> And the people blessed all the men who volunteered
> to live in Jerusalem. (v. 2)

It's this last group that gets our attention; these are the first of the "willing unknowns" of our story. This verse isn't referring to the people who had lost the toss of the dice. The word that is translated "volunteered" is from the Hebrew word *nadab*, which means "to impel, to incite from within." The word implies the idea of generosity and willingness.[2] If you've ever moved, you know the significance of their action. It meant uprooting their families, packing up their belongings, and building new homes on lots covered with tumbled-down structures and weeds. And that was before there were any such things as moving vans or landscape architects!

The Willing Unknowns in Nehemiah 11

As we move through chapter 11, we find five groups of willing unknowns. The first group is the one we've already noticed, *the people who volunteered to move.* We find the second group when we

2. The word *nadab* is used many times in the Old Testament. Exodus 35 gives us a clear picture of its meaning as it describes the people who put together the tabernacle —people skilled in craftsmanship, embroidery, weaving, to name a few areas—who gave of their substance, talent, and time for the service of God. Yet not one name of that crew is recorded or remembered.

glance down to verses 10–12a. They are some of those who already lived in the city, *people who worked within the temple.*

> From the priests: Jedaiah the son of Joiarib, Jachin, Seraiah the son of Hilkiah, the son of Meshullam, the son of Zadok, the son of Meraioth, the son of Ahitub, the leader of the house of God, *and their kinsmen who performed the work of the temple, 822.* (emphasis added)

Talk about a big church! Eight hundred and twenty-two—that's quite a staff. And not one of them named specifically. You can bet that a good percentage of them did jobs that most people took for granted, like dusting and lighting lamps and running errands. They served anonymously and without glory so that God's people could be blessed.

There was a third group as well, *those who worked outside the place of worship.*

> Now from the Levites: Shemaiah the son of Hasshub, the son of Azrikam, the son of Hashabiah, the son of Bunni; and Shabbethai and Jozabad, from the leaders of the Levites, who were in charge of the outside work of the house of God. (vv. 15–16)

The phrase "in charge of the outside work" referred to two types of tasks: the maintenance of the exterior beauty of the temple and the grounds around it, and work such as judging and counseling people. Jobs of ministry outside the temple walls.

The fourth group of people was made up of *those who supported the ministry through prayer.*

> And Mattaniah the son of Mica, the son of Zabdi, the son of Asaph, who was the leader in beginning the thanksgiving at prayer, and Bakbukiah, the second among his brethren; and Abda the son of Shammua, the son of Galal, the son of Jeduthun. (v. 17)

Ever heard of Mattaniah? It's unlikely. He probably couldn't preach worth anything, but he could pray. And it was probably his prayers that kept that temple alive.

The fifth group of people was *those who served the Lord with singing.*

> Now the overseer of the Levites in Jerusalem was Uzzi the son of Bani, the son of Hashabiah, the son of Mattaniah, the son of Mica, from the sons of Asaph, who were the singers for the service of the house of

God. For there was a commandment from the king concerning them and a firm regulation for the song leaders day by day. (vv. 22–23)

This was no last-minute quartet; it was a group of committed musicians who willingly developed their gifts and gave of their time as a ministry to the people.

Practical Principles for Today

Why spend a whole lesson studying a bunch of people nobody's ever heard of, whose names we'll never remember? Because almost all of us struggle at times with our self-esteem. Almost every one of us at times wonders if it would make any difference at all if we were not on this earth, or what conceivable value there is in our seemingly small talents. It's from this unpronounceable passage of Scripture that we can draw three encouraging principles.

First: *Your gift makes you valuable, if not necessarily popular.* If you are gifted in an area that never reaches the spotlight, don't worry about it. You are as valuable as Mattaniah or Uzzi, and you are just as well-known to God.

Second: *Every labor done in love is remembered by God, never forgotten.* Listen to Hebrews 6:10.

God is not unjust so as to forget your work and the love which you have shown toward His name, in having ministered and in still ministering to the saints.

Third: *Our final rewards will be determined on the basis of personal faithfulness, not public applause.* The public may never know of your ministry, whether it takes place in the privacy of your prayer closet or on the back row of the choir. But God will not reward you according to the number of appreciation plaques on your wall or thank-you notes in your scrapbook. He will reward you according to the pure-hearted service of your life.

Can you put your desire for recognition aside and say with Yohana Omari, the first African bishop in Tanzania, these simple, humble words?

"I want to be like the little donkey our Lord chose to ride on to enter Jerusalem. They laid their robes on it and shouted, but the shouting was all for the Lord Jesus whom he was carrying."[3]

3. As quoted by Ruth A. Tucker in *Sacred Stories*, p. 13.

🍇 Living Insights

Jedaiah, Mattaniah, Shemiah . . . did you make it through those tongue-twisting lists?

There are probably a few unknown, if not unpronounceable, names right within your own church body today, serving just as faithfully and anonymously as these people we've been reading about. Do you know who they are? Do you find yourself taking your temperature-controlled sanctuary or your spic-and-span hallways for granted? Someone had to set that thermostat and polish those floors. How about the decorations that brighten up the holiday services, or the people who take up the offering and tally attendance?

Take some time this Sunday to look beyond the surface. Whose quiet jobs make your worship time run a little smoother? It's likely that they get discouraged from time to time, occasionally even feel unappreciated. Why not drop a note in the mail, or a whispered thank-you in someone's ear? List a few people below whose names or jobs come immediately to mind.

_____

_____

_____

There are a lot of little jobs that make a big difference. Make sure they get recognized!

🍇 Living Insights

Since there are only a few up-front people in every congregation, chances are you've done a seemingly mundane job at some point in your life . . . passing out songbooks, rounding up the coffee maker, praying for a youth rally. And maybe because those jobs generally go unappreciated, you've not appreciated yourself enough. Maybe you've even felt you had little to contribute to the body of Christ.

But as we saw in our study today, there were 822 people working in the temple of Jerusalem who probably felt similarly from time to time, yet without them the temple would have been a different place. Spend some time looking up the following passages of Scripture. What do they have to say about your significance in God's kingdom?

1 Corinthians 12: _All roles are_
important yet different

Ephesians 4:7–13: _____

Now look up Colossians 3:23–24. What does this passage have to say about our attitude toward the tasks we've been given?
Do everything "as to the Lord =
knowing that God will reward
you.

Chapter 15

HAPPINESS IS
A WALK ON THE WALL
Nehemiah 12

In November of 1989, while Americans prepared to celebrate Thanksgiving, East Germans were celebrating an unforgettable moment of thanksgiving of their own. The wall which had for so long kept them incarcerated in a communist regime was finally coming down. The power of the old-guard party leaders had developed too many cracks and had begun to crumble. Along with that ruling power tumbled its symbol—the Berlin Wall—almost as quickly and unexpectedly as it was put up in August 1961. Amidst the rubble there were mass hysterics of cheering, dancing, singing, hugging, and crying, in a celebration that was heard around the world.

A festive scene almost identical to this twentieth-century phenomenon occurred thousands of years ago in Nehemiah's day. The joyous sights and sounds of those East Germans rings forth like a clarion echo of the sights and sounds reverberating in Nehemiah 12. Only that time, the celebration was centered around a wall being raised up, not torn down.

Dedication of the Wall

Behind Jerusalem's broad, well-constructed wall, a renewed vision was bringing fresh signs of growth to a barren city. Commerce was beginning to bud again, homes were sprouting up, and an influx of new people was bringing back a healthy flush to a city awakening from a long winter's sleep.

Today, Nehemiah is going to take us to a springtime celebration in Jerusalem—the gala dedication of the wall surrounding Jerusalem.

Preliminary Factors

After a long pause swollen with the names of people and places (Neh. 11:3–12:26), Nehemiah resumes the movement of his narrative with preparations for the dedication ceremony.

> Now at the dedication of the wall of Jerusalem [Nehemiah and Ezra] sought out the Levites from all their places, to bring them to Jerusalem. (v. 27a)

108

In order for these two leaders to pull off this celebration, they needed the help of a group of men known as Levites. But recruiting these men was no simple task of making a few phone calls. According to Nehemiah 11:18, it meant contacting 284 men in Jerusalem, besides all those who still lived outside the city! Why was it necessary to reach all these men? Because they were the descendants of Levi, specialists in temple and tabernacle activities. And if the wall was to be dedicated for the glory of God, these were the men who should head up that process.

Now these priests weren't some somber, joyless group of men who sat silently in the same temple seat every week. According to the rest of 12:27, they were brought to Jerusalem to "celebrate the dedication with gladness, with hymns of thanksgiving and with songs to the accompaniment of cymbals, harps, and lyres." This was one merry bunch! It even included a special group made up of "the sons of the singers" (v. 28)—probably a special singing ensemble selected from among these Levitical families charged with passing on the sacred songs of Israel's faith.

Before these celebrations began, however, a time was set aside for purification.

> And the priests and the Levites purified themselves;
> they also purified the people, the gates, and the wall.
> (v. 30)

How did they do that? We're not told exactly. But more than likely it had to do with sin offerings made on behalf of the people. Before the celebration of the wall could begin, before it could be enjoyed without reservation, the people's hearts needed to be pure, cleansed through the confession of sin.

Procedure

Next, Nehemiah explains how he organized the celebration.

> Then I had the leaders of Judah come up on top
> of the wall, and I appointed two great choirs, the first
> proceeding to the right on top of the wall toward the
> Refuse Gate. . . .
> The second choir proceeded to the left, while I
> followed them with half of the people on the wall,
> above the Tower of Furnaces, to the Broad Wall.
> (vv. 31, 38)

Can you imagine? Dozens, perhaps even hundreds, of singers and musicians clambered onto the new wall, grouping themselves together for last-minute voice and instrument tunings as the celebration started.[1]

Finally, the bands struck up, the choirs sang, and Ezra and Nehemiah went rejoicing along the sturdy wall, trampling underfoot the scoff of their enemies: "If a fox should jump on it, he would break their stone wall down!" (Neh. 4:3).

Praise

🏵 When these divided troupes met back together in the temple court, a joy reigned that is almost unparalleled in all of Scripture.

> And on that day they offered great sacrifices and rejoiced because God had given them great joy, even the women and children rejoiced, so that the joy of Jerusalem was heard from afar. (12:43)

Dedication of the People

Besides dedicating the wall to the Lord that day, the people also committed themselves to supporting the priests and the Levites financially and to keeping consecrated lives.

Dedication of Money

> On that day men were also appointed over the chambers for the stores, the contributions, the first fruits, and the tithes, to gather into them from the fields of the cities the portions required by the law for the priests and Levites; for Judah rejoiced over the priests and Levites who served. . . . And so all Israel in the days of Zerubbabel and Nehemiah gave the portions due the singers and the gatekeepers as each day required, and set apart the consecrated portion for the Levites, and the Levites set apart the consecrated portion for the sons of Aaron. (vv. 44, 47)

The prevailing spirit of joy encouraged the people to give without any resentment to the needs of those appointed to oversee the temple.

Consecration of Their Lives

> For [the priests and Levites] performed the worship of their God and the service of purification, together

---

1. There were several instruments used in this Mardi Gras of praise and dedication. The cymbals used were much like cymbals used today, held in the hands and crashed together. The harps were perhaps more like glorified mandolins, instruments with bell-shaped ends and several strings. The lyres were easily portable instruments with two arms joined at the top by a cross piece, having strings all roughly the same length.

110

with the singers and the gatekeepers in accordance
with the command of David and of his son Solomon.
For in the days of David and Asaph, in ancient times,
there were leaders of the singers, songs of praise and
hymns of thanksgiving to God. (vv. 45–46)

It reads like the end of a fairy tale. In the midst of their ceremony
of consecration there was a balance of truth and emotion, words
and song.

Four Vital Conclusions

No one who saw or heard the boisterous cheers and praise of the
Israelites that day would have had any doubts about the vibrancy of
their faith. Let's take a moment to examine the vibrancy of our own
faith with these four applications.

*An atmosphere of happiness should surround God's people when they
are together.* One of the most magnetic and powerful forces in any
local ministry is the presence of joy. Do you contribute to this or
detract from it? Do you genuinely enjoy getting together with other
believers to offer up praise in singing? Are you enjoyable to be
around, or do you give off a signal that you'd rather not be bothered
by people? There ought to be an atmosphere of joy every time Christians are together.

Proverbs 15:13 says, "A joyful heart makes a cheerful face, But
when the heart is sad, the spirit is broken." Happiness is a matter
of the heart that can easily be shared with a smile, a spirit of enthusiasm, or a willingness to participate.

Music is one of the most expressive ways to communicate happiness.
You would be hard-pressed to find a genuinely happy Christian who
didn't enjoy either participating in or listening to music. Music has
been given by God to enhance the joy of a worship service and the
hearts of Christians. It is one of the most expressive ways we can
communicate happiness. Why? Because "music short-circuits the
senses with a direct pathway into human emotion."[2] Perhaps this is
one of the reasons why the apostle Paul urges all Christians not to

get drunk with wine, for that is dissipation, but be
filled with the Spirit, speaking to one another in psalms
and hymns and spiritual songs, singing and making
melody with your heart to the Lord. (Eph. 5:18–19)

2. Philip Yancey, *Open Windows* (Westchester, Ill.: Crossway Books, 1982), p. 154.

In his book, *Open Windows*, Philip Yancey reflects on this power-ful vehicle that not only allows us to express happiness but fosters it in our hearts as well. After listening to the Chicago Symphony Chorus perform Beethoven's *Missa Solemnis*, he penned these words:

> Fortunately for the unbelievers of the Chorus these highly charged words of grace are neatly packaged in rhythmic Latin phrases that glissade safely off the tongue. Yet as I watch, something approaching miracle seems to occur. A Jewish tenor on the third row, who stiffened up for this performance with three Manhat-tans and a pack of Camels, who gives not a rip for "the only begotten Son of God," whose chin is marked with styptic pencil and collar flecked with blood from a hasty shave—that tenor's face is transformed. Harsh-ness drains from it; he sucks a deep breath of hope and release from the anxious world offstage and belts out "Agnus dei, Agnus dei" ("Lamb of God, who takest away the sins of the world, have mercy upon us") as though it is the one true plea he has ever made. Per-haps, for a moment, he does mean it.[3]

A joyful spirit will have far-reaching effects. What was it that was "heard from afar" when the great choirs sang atop the temple walls (Neh. 12:43) . . . the singing? The instruments? No, it was "the joy of Jerusalem." Even for all the money and equipment spent and used today to deliver the Christian message, there is still no TV station or radio tower that can match the sending power of Christians ex-hibiting God's joy on a day-to-day basis.

Joy is not dependent upon outward circumstances, but upon inward focus. If you doubt this, look at the circumstances surrounding the Israelites before, during, and after their celebration. They were still under Persian authority, living in a city filled with rubble, unceas-ingly hounded by outside enemies who opposed them. But these same people celebrated with a joy that practically shook the homes of their critics. Why? Because they had their focus centered com-pletely around Jehovah.

3. Yancey, *Open Windows*, p. 150.

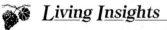

Living Insights

STUDY ONE

Joy is not dependent on outward circumstances.

Now that's a tough truth to hang onto in the face of all the difficulties we run into daily. Most of us have become experts at trying to control our circumstances and other people in order to secure our own happiness. Yet the harder we try, the more frustrated, angry, and depressed we become when things don't go the way we planned.

Dr. Larry Crabb, in *Effective Biblical Counseling,* offers this advice:

> Many of us place top priority not on becoming Christ like in the middle of our problems but on finding happiness. I want to be happy but the paradoxical truth is that I will never be happy if I am concerned primarily with becoming happy. My overriding goal must be in every circumstance to respond biblically, to put the Lord first, to seek to behave as He would want me to. The wonderful truth is that as we devote all our energies to the task of becoming what Christ wants us to be, He fills us with joy unspeakable and a peace far surpassing what the world offers. . . .
>
> Paul said it was his ambition (goal) not to become happy but to please God at every moment. What a transforming thought! When I drive my car to work and someone cuts me off, when my kids act up during church, when the dishwasher breaks—my primary responsibility is to *please God!*[4]

Do you need to give up pursuing happiness and instead devote all that mental, emotional, and physical energy to pursuing God? If you make this change in your focus, say hello to joy for me.

Living Insights

STUDY TWO

In his commentary on the book of John, William Barclay says,

> We are chosen for *joy.* However hard the Christian way is, it is, both in the travelling and in the goal, the way of joy. There is always a joy in doing the right thing.

---

4. Lawrence J. Crabb, Jr., *Effective Biblical Counseling* (Grand Rapids, Mich.: Zondervan Publishing House, 1977), pp. 20–21.

When we have evaded some duty or some task, when at last we set our hand to it, joy comes to us. The Christian is the man of joy; the Christian is the laughing cavalier of Christ. A gloomy Christian is a contradiction in terms, and nothing in all religious history has done Christianity more harm than its connection with black clothes and long faces.[5]

According to Nehemiah 12:43, "The joy of Jerusalem was heard from afar." How far is your joy heard? Is it seen in your home? At your job? When you are worshiping together with other Christians? Can the people around you who don't know Christ sense it?

What do your answers tell you about the level of joy in your life? If you would like to know more about where your joy can come from, read John 15:1–11.

Joy of Christ remain in you

5. William Barclay, *The Gospel of John*, The Daily Study Bible Series, 2d ed. (Philadelphia, Pa.: Westminster Press, 1956), vol. 2, pp. 206–7.

Chapter 16

TAKING PROBLEMS
BY THE THROAT

Nehemiah 13

Ludwig van Beethoven has been described as the "musician who felt, thought, and dreamt in tones."[1] By the age of five he was playing the violin. At thirteen he was on his way to becoming an accomplished organist. In his early twenties he made his public debut as a concert pianist, playing his own concerto major.

Elizabeth Brentano once reported in a letter that Beethoven likened music to wine and saw himself as "the Bacchus who presses out this glorious wine for mankind."[2] And press out music he did— nine symphonies, five concertos, and countless overtures, minuets, chamber pieces, and sonatas.

In contrast to the great heights of his professional success, Beethoven's personal life was marked with great depths of suffering. He moved from living under the shadow of a father described as "a shiftless, feebly unscrupulous man" . . . who tried "to exploit Beethoven as an infant prodigy"[3] to living with one of the darkest of catastrophic ironies—the loss of his hearing. In a letter dated June 1, 1801, the thirty-one-year-old musical genius vented his rage over this staggering blow.

> "Your Beethoven is most unhappy," he writes, "and at strife with nature and Creator. I have often cursed the latter for exposing his creatures to the merest accident, so that often the most beautiful buds are broken or destroyed thereby. Only think that my noblest faculty, my hearing, has greatly deteriorated."[4]

But Beethoven channeled his intense anger into an indomitable determination to continue composing, which was summed up in his

---

1. J. W. N. Sullivan, *Beethoven: His Spiritual Development* (New York, N.Y.: New American Library of World Literature, Mentor Books, 1949), p. 69.

2. As quoted by Sullivan in *Beethoven*, p. 9.

3. Sullivan, *Beethoven*, pp. 44, 46.

4. Ludwig van Beethoven, as quoted by Sullivan in *Beethoven*, p. 59.

words, "I will take Fate by the throat."[5] The louder the silence roared in his ears, the more richly and intensely the music flowed from Beethoven's heart. And those glorious sounds intoxicated the world.

Another individual also refused to let problems conquer him—Nehemiah. This cupbearer, construction foreman, and governor, intensely desiring to please the Lord, took Israel's sin by the throat wherever he found it. Throughout our study we have seen him ward off enemies and press out a glorious spirit of revival in the lackadaisical Jews. But nowhere is his indomitable spirit more clearly seen than in chapter 13, where he squeezes the life out of four serious problems.

Problems in Nehemiah's Day

Nehemiah's time in Jerusalem was amazingly fruitful, but he was honor-bound to return to his former position as cupbearer to King Artaxerxes (see Neh. 2:6). Nehemiah 13:6 tells us that he was away from Jerusalem for some time before asking permission to return; but because the time reference in the verse is ambiguous, we don't know exactly how long he was gone. However long, though, it was long enough for the children of Israel to get themselves into some serious trouble—the kind of trouble that could eventually deafen the ears of their whole nation to the words of the Lord.

A Compromising Companionship

The first problem involved an Israelite priest who offered part of the temple as a private hotel suite for one of Jerusalem's worst enemies.

> Now prior to this, Eliashib the priest, who was appointed over the chambers of the house of our God, being related to Tobiah, had prepared a large room for him, where formerly they put the grain offerings, the frankincense, the utensils, and the tithes of grain, wine and oil prescribed for the Levites, the singers and the gatekeepers, and the contributions for the priests. (vv. 4–5)

Tobiah had been an opponent of the rebuilding project from the beginning. Yet while Nehemiah was away, this man wormed his way not just behind the walls of the city, but inside the most sacred walls in Jerusalem—the temple. And the high priest, Eliashib, allowed it.

Action taken. When Nehemiah came back and discovered what had taken place, he stormed through the temple and did some serious spring cleaning.

5. Beethoven, as quoted by Sullivan in *Beethoven*, p. 62.

And I came to Jerusalem and learned about the evil
that Eliashib had done for Tobiah, by preparing a room
for him in the courts of the house of God. And it was
very displeasing to me, so I threw all of Tobiah's household goods out of the room. Then I gave an order and
they cleansed the rooms; and I returned there the uten-
sils of the house of God with the grain offerings and
the frankincense. (vv. 7–9)

Nehemiah's response was swift and decisive. Looking back on
it, as we are now, there is little doubt that he did the right thing.
But there were undoubtedly some there that day who thought
Nehemiah was overreacting, being unreasonable. Fortunately for
Israel, Nehemiah wasn't interested in winning any popularity con-
tests. His only interest was in cleaning out the evil that was already
affecting the people's ability to hear and obey the Word of the Lord.

A Financial Fiasco

Perhaps it was the outrage of finding one of Israel's worst enemies
living in the temple that prompted Nehemiah to do more probing
under the beds and into the closets of Israel's state of affairs. He
didn't have to look very long before he came across more grime.

I also discovered that the portions of the Levites
had not been given them, so that the Levites and the
singers who performed the service had gone away, each
to his own field. (v. 10)

According to the Law of Moses, the Levites were to minister in
and around the temple and the people were to support them through
tithes. But because the tithes had ceased, the Levites had all gone
back to their farms, and there was nothing but silence where there
once had been ministry.

Action taken. Again Nehemiah took the situation by the throat.

So I reprimanded the officials and said, "Why is the
house of God forsaken?" Then I gathered them together and restored them to their posts. All Judah
then brought the tithe of the grain, wine, and oil into
the storehouses. And in charge of the storehouses I
appointed Shelemiah the priest, Zadok the scribe, and
Pedaiah of the Levites, and in addition to them was
Hanan the son of Zaccur, the son of Mattaniah; for
they were considered reliable, and it was their task to
distribute to their kinsmen. Remember me for this, O
my God, and do not blot out my loyal deeds which I

117

have performed for the house of my God and its services. (vv. 11–14)

In Ecclesiastes 3, Solomon says "There is an appointed time for everything. A time to give birth, and a time to die . . . A time to be silent, and a time to speak" (vv. 1a, 2a, 7b). From Nehemiah's example, we might add, "there's a time to pray, and a time to take problems by the throat." Nehemiah knew when and how to do both. He knew when to wait on the Lord in prayer, and he knew when to get up off his knees and confront.

A Secularized Sabbath

The third serious problem to catch Nehemiah's attention and raise his ire was the people's lack of concern for keeping the Sabbath.

> In those days I saw in Judah some who were treading wine presses on the sabbath, and bringing in sacks of grain and loading them on donkeys, as well as wine, grapes, figs, and all kinds of loads, and they brought them into Jerusalem on the sabbath day. So I admonished them on the day they sold food. Also men of Tyre were living there who imported fish and all kinds of merchandise, and sold them to the sons of Judah on the sabbath, even in Jerusalem. (vv. 15–16)

According to the Jewish calendar, the Sabbath—Saturday—was to be a day of rest, in observance of the example set by the Lord when He rested after creating the world. This practice was not only written in the Law of Moses but was part of the covenant these people signed in Nehemiah 10:31. Yet they had gone back to conducting business as usual. No holy Sabbath, no spiritual distinction in their weekly schedule, no fulfillment of their promise. Only a people who could hear a bargain from a mile away, but who were stone deaf to God's commands concerning the Sabbath.

Action taken. Nehemiah hadn't forgotten the people's promise, and he wasn't about to let them forget it either.

> Then I reprimanded the nobles of Judah and said to them, "What is this evil thing you are doing, by profaning the sabbath day? Did not your fathers do the same so that our God brought on us, and on this city, all this trouble? Yet you are adding to the wrath on Israel by profaning the sabbath."
> And it came about that just as it grew dark at the gates of Jerusalem before the sabbath, I commanded that the doors should be shut and that they should not

open them until after the sabbath. Then I stationed some of my servants at the gates that no load should enter on the sabbath day. Once or twice the traders and merchants of every kind of merchandise spent the night outside Jerusalem. Then I warned them and said to them, "Why do you spend the night in front of the wall? If you do so again, I will use force against you." From that time on they did not come on the sabbath. And I commanded the Levites that they should purify themselves and come as gatekeepers to sanctify the sabbath day. For this also remember me, O my God, and have compassion on me according to the greatness of Thy lovingkindness." (vv. 17–22)

There was nothing indecisive about Nehemiah. He went for the jugular vein on sinful practices and didn't relinquish his grip until the life had been completely squeezed out of them.

A Domestic Disobedience

The final problem that Nehemiah encountered was perhaps the most dangerous and most difficult to deal with—the Jews were inter-marrying with the pagan people around them. The result was the mixing not only of blood, but of languages and beliefs as well.

In those days I also saw that the Jews had married women from Ashdod, Ammon, and Moab. As for their children, half spoke in the language of Ashdod, and none of them was able to speak the language of Judah, but the language of his own people. (vv. 23–24)

Israel was raising a generation of children who could not speak or understand the language of the Scriptures—this was a problem that threatened to wipe out Israel's ability to hear the voice of the Lord.

Action taken. Like Beethoven, the greater the problem, the greater the intensity with which Nehemiah responded.

So I contended with them and cursed them and struck some of them and pulled out their hair, and made them swear by God, "You shall not give your daughters to their sons, nor take of their daughters for your sons or for yourselves." (v. 25)

There are few stronger passages in the Bible concerning confron-tation. When it says that Nehemiah "cursed" them, it doesn't mean he used profanity. The word *curse* means "to treat with contempt,

119

to revile"; it's a very severe term. The verse also says that Nehemiah "pulled out their hair;" the word *pulled* means "to make slick or polished" and is used mainly for plucking out part of the beard. Israel's situation was becoming desperate, so Nehemiah responded with desperate measures (see also vv. 26–30).

An Analysis of the Solution

Nehemiah followed four basic steps as he dealt with Israel's problems. First, *he faced the sin head on*. Second, *he condemned it severely*. Third, *he worked toward a permanent correction*. Fourth, *he followed the situation up with prayer.*

Problems in Our Day

Let's take a moment to look at three principles from our lesson today that can help strangle the problems in our own lives.

First: *Dealing with problems begins with honest observation.* You cannot solve a problem that you haven't identified. We must force ourselves to face the truth of our compromising alliances, areas of selfishness, failure to keep our word . . . no matter how painful the truth.

Second: *Correcting what is honestly observed demands fearless conviction.* Thousands of fears keep us from confronting problems—the fear of what others will think or say, the fear of upsetting the status quo, the fear of being misunderstood. Yet we must meet the challenge of Joshua 24:15—

> If it is disagreeable in your sight to serve the Lord, choose for yourselves today whom you will serve . . . as for me and my house, we will serve the Lord.

Third: *Honest observation and fearless conviction must be tempered by consistent devotion.* Nehemiah seemed to be constantly dealing with major problems, but he didn't become bitter or revengeful. His constant prayers and focus on the Lord kept him from becoming a harsh, irritating, severe, condemning critic and gave him the tempering power that only comes from God.

We all have sins that we have allowed to visit from time to time and have finally invited back to stay—and those are the things in our lives that we need to take by the throat and throw out. But getting rid of those unwanted guests will not be easy. Once you serve them notice to get off the premises, you can expect them to put up a fight. They'll threaten you with every fear they can muster. They'll woo you with every rationalization they can whisper. They'll even go so far as to hire some leg-breakers like guilt, depression, anxiety, and anger to work you over.

But remember one thing. As a believer, your body is a temple of God. And no sin can stay in that temple if you're willing to throw it out, as Nehemiah did Tobiah.

Take some time to concentrate on an enemy guest in your temple that needs to be evicted.

Honest observation. If you were to focus on only one area of disobedience that needs to be changed in your life, what would it be?

_____agape_____

_____

Fearless conviction. Are you willing to be committed to pleasing God in this area, no matter what the cost?

Deep devotion. What Scriptures, books, tapes, friends can you lean on for help with this particular problem? Are you spending enough time with God? No I

_____

_____

_____

Most of us need to slow down and give all the biblical truths we're learning time to sink down deep into our hearts. Why don't you set aside some uninterrupted time to go back over each of the chapters and the Living Insights in this study and record on the following page the important truths that God has shown you.

Nehemiah: Man of the Hour _Erect spiritual walls and repair those walls – via prayer and dependence upon God_

Nehemiah on His Knees _Are you listening to the Savior? Pray._

Preparation for a Mighty Task _Opposition can sometimes be an affirmation that we are in God's will_

Motivation: The Basis of Leadership _I need to sharpen my focus on Christ when I am being criticized_

Knocked Down, but not Knocked Out _____

Discouragement: Its Cause and Cure _____

Love, Loans, and Money Problems _____

How to Handle a Promotion _____

Operation Intimidation _____

BOOKS FOR
PROBING FURTHER

There's a real shortage today of leaders who are built out of the bricklike qualities of Nehemiah. Seems like a lot of folks want to cut corners and use lighter materials so they can be recognized quicker and at less cost to themselves. It's true, bricks aren't as easy to work with as hay and sticks because they're heavy and more expensive. But in the long run, they're worth it.

For further help in constructing your own leadership qualities, here are a few books we'd like to recommend.

Barber, Cyril J. *Nehemiah and the Dynamics of Effective Leadership*. Neptune, N.J.: Loizeaux Brothers, 1976. Written as a practical devotional commentary, this book takes us through Nehemiah passage by passage, teaching us how to plan our work, organize our time and resources, motivate others, set realistic goals, and handle many other down-to-earth issues.

Blue, Ron. *Master Your Money*. Nashville, Tenn.: Thomas Nelson Publishers, 1986. In this helpful book, the author has combined the Bible's timeless teachings on stewardship and responsibility with the most modern insights on financial management and cash control.

Friesen, Garry. *Decision Making and the Will of God*. Portland, Oreg.: Multnomah Press, 1980. In an easy-to-follow narrative style, Friesen carefully examines today's traditional view of how to discern God's will. In contrast, he presents a view he considers more biblical, by which every leader will benefit by wrestling with.

Hansel, Tim. *Eating Problems for Breakfast*. Dallas, Tex.: Word Publishing, 1988. The author believes that problems are an unavoidable, necessary ingredient of the abundant life, which therefore have to be defined and dealt with. In this book, he offers methods to help you accurately identify and creatively resolve many of the problems that fling themselves across your path.

Sanders, J. Oswald. *Spiritual Leadership*. Chicago, Ill: Moody Press, 1980. Already a Christian classic, this book emphasizes character, passion, and godliness as the foundations of leadership. It is thoughtfully and practically written, expounding timeless principles drawn from the whole of Scripture.

Swindoll, Charles R. *Hand Me Another Brick.* Nashville, Tenn.: Thomas Nelson Publishers, 1978. Paralleling our study guide and radio broadcast series, this book is designed to teach you principles of effective leadership and help you learn how to motivate yourself and others.

Tozer, A. W. *The Knowledge of the Holy.* Jubilee edition. New York, N.Y.: Harper and Row, Publishers, 1975. A classic on Christian devotion, this book discusses the attributes of God in words that go straight to the heart. Informative as well as inspirational, it restores the biblical concept of God to the center of our attention.

White, John. *Excellence in Leadership.* Downers Grove, Ill.: Inter-Varsity Press, 1986. The author confronts the crises facing leaders today, giving us a model for surmounting problems and overcoming obstacles with wisdom and biblical insight.

———. *Daring to Draw Near.* Downers Grove, Ill.: InterVarsity Press, 1977. By showing us some of the prayers of the Bible, the author teaches us about praying ourselves. We also learn about the God to whom we pray—the one who desires communication with us, the one who takes the initiative.